Cash Operations Management

Cash Operations Management:

Profits from Within

Gerald R. Sinn

PBI
a petrocelli
book
new york / princeton

All of the case histories used in this book are true and are taken from factual accounts in the author's files. In most instances, names of companies, individuals, and products have been changed to protect the identity of the companies and the privacy of the individuals connected with these companies.

Library of Congress Cataloging in Publication Data
Sinn, Gerald R.
    Cash operations management.
    Bibliography: p.
    Includes index.
    1. Cash management. I. Title.
HG4028.C45S53   658.1'5244   80-20896
ISBN 0-89433-116-7

To my wife Marilyn,
whose loving patience
has paved my way
over the years and
my son and daughter
Gregory and Jana Lee

Contents

Preface

Cash Operations Management is about cash profits and operations management, and the ways to improve them. It gives the reader better insight into profits lost through the distribution of dollars in modern business organizations.

This is also an inflation-fighting book, in that it concentrates on reducing the price of a product in today's market, in addition to getting more production out of the business dollar. The book furnishes case histories from my files, through which the reader can obtain an extended, in-depth approach to obtaining cash profits that are often overlooked. It may not provide an instant, overall solution, but it will raise questions that can yield profitable answers. In today's inflationary economy, this new method for increasing profits should prove useful in solving numerous business problems.

This book is designed to explain how important parts of a business operation are ignored because they seem not to involve dynamic management interests or to carry project titles such as product mix, purchase variances, sales projections, and so on. Emphasis is placed on areas that steal cash from systems, with the expectation of recovering lost cash and putting a stop to future cash losses by improving systems and procedures.

Cash Operations Management covers nearly every area in a business organization that has profit problems at one time or another. The reader who is looking for an immediate method of improving profits in his or her business will find that the cash systems program outlined in this book will:

— bridge the financial-communications gap among the parts of an organization

— reveal a specialized cash-management system with the potential of opening vast profit areas never anticipated by management people

— more than ever before, reveal how a management consultant goes about finding additional profits

— take top executives out of their offices and show them what is really happening on the production-plant floor

— not favor monthly financial statements as method for finding new, high-potential profits.

— go beyond the areas in systems and procedures where auditors look for profits

— show how obtaining profits from within a business organization can relieve inflationary pressures

Acknowledgments

This book might not have been written if it hadn't been for the encouragement of my friend of twenty years, Herman "Mac" McDaniel. I thank him many times over for his enduring persistence.

Also I wish to thank my copy editor, Mrs. Charesse V. Haas.

1. The Inflation Fighter

At the end of January 1974 the price of styrene monomer was 7¢ per pound. On the first day of February the price of this raw material, which is used in the manufacture of phonograph records, jumped 27 percent. By October 1974 it had spiraled to 25¢ a pound, an incredible 257-percent price increase in a matter of eight months. A few months later the consumer price for a long-play record began to rise.

This price rise was no accident. The February 1974 price increase coincided with President Nixon's announcement that the Cost of Living Council had lifted price regulations on certain raw materials. The "price freeze" of 1973 was over; the horrendous price-inflation spiral that descended on the nation, however, had only just begun. Acting with haste and greed, American business increased prices on American consumer goods as if there were no tomorrow.

It seemed that overnight, suppliers of raw materials in every field wanted price increases for their products. Federal investigations may have exposed some of the reason for this devastating change in the U.S. economy, but no agency—the President or anyone else—would attempt to stop the inflation. Instead of improving the country's economic position, their actions caused it to worsen when, in June 1974, for example, Congress voted to increase the national debt.

Later in 1975, after the greatest damage had been done, the aluminum industry was criticized by Washington for putting through a 30-percent increase. Ironically, aluminum held its price while other companies were hitting their customers with increases of up to 100 percent. The government simply was not responding adequately to pressures.

A Price-Control Ceiling

The absurdity of what occurred to the American economy in 1974, regarding the price of industrial raw materials, just was not within reason. The government should have felt the intense inflationary pressures stirring at the time they lifted price and wage controls. But no responsible moves were taken to stop the inflation.

The oil companies had recently shocked their customers in the price of a gallon of gasoline—and they got away with it. Now, when controls were lifted, other industries saw the opportunity to do the same. This was the time for the government to institute limited price controls.

American industry and commerce could have gotten along with an inflation factor of 2 to 5 percent in 1975. If limited controls on prices had been imposed, two years would have been adequate time to stop the panic among America's business people. Our free enterprise system would have settled down and been free to work in a normal business-related atmosphere.

A New Cash Operations System

Today the American business person carries the heavy burden of inflation. There is the tool of price increase, but now the other side of business takes on a new importance. There must be belt tightening; businesses must educate themselves to the increased cost of doing business. They must find an inflation-fighter program.

Now, more than at any other time in our nation's economic history, there is an urgent need for an industrial and commercial inflation-fighter program. This book has been written to meet the purpose of such a program. It outlines a program of cash operations management that has already proved successful in business organizations.

The book introduces a *cash management system* that goes to the source: where the decision is made to spend the profit dollar. It challenges the vendor to prove that a product is worth the price charged. It asks the vendor to cross-examine his or her supplier about price validity.

The cash operations management system is intended to bridge many communication gaps in industry. It is a program needed by every type of business organization that receives and distributes cash in significant amounts.

2 A Cash-Profits System

On a balmy, overcast Wednesday afternoon in October 1972 I walked up the circular drive to a brick canopy in front of the Coilcraft Corporation building. The company was located in the countryside just outside the small town of Cary, Illinois.

The trip that had brought me here that afternoon had taken years. My business experience had exposed me to both large and small industrial corporations all across the United States.

Everything seemed right. The weather was mild, with no wind. I was confident. I had prepared for this day with years of business experience. Before entering the building I paused a moment under the accented Spanish canopy. As I took a deep breath of fresh air, I caught a glimpse of the countryside. A small red barn across the road, and cows grazing in a pasture in the distance, added serenity to the scene.

I walked into the lobby and handed the receptionist my newly prepared calling card. I had no appointment and hadn't expected to see the company president that day. The receptionist glanced at the card.

"Your company is 'Cash Management Through Operations'?" she asked, reading the notation on my card.

"No," I replied. "I'm a management consultant. Cash management through operations is the type of work I do for companies."

The receptionist immediately picked up a phone and dialed the president of Coilcraft. He consented to see me without an appointment. It would be the first presentation of my cash operations management program.

Start-Up of the Cash Operations Management System

I was somewhat surprised that Charles Liebman called me into his office so soon, and I was somewhat nervous. He offered me a chair. It was comfortable, brown leather and chrome. His modern office decor reflected the decoration pattern of the chair. Liebman was a pleasant, handsome man, probably in his late forties. An authentic executive.

"Mr. Sinn," he asked, "what kind of a program is cash management through operations?"

It wasn't necessary to oversell him. I simply had to convey the truth about what I hoped to do for his business.

"Mr. Liebman, I'm starting a consulting practice that will have the sole purpose of bringing lost cash back into businesses. The term "through operations" means that I will find this money deep in the operational areas of your plants and offices."

It was as simple as that. For most of my business career—and, I'm sure, like many other business executives—I had operated on the premise that to acquire business profits was complicated, functional, and laborious. That's not altogether wrong, but there *is* another approach.

"My plan for finding cash in your company, Mr. Liebman," I continued, "is to begin with something as simple as an accounts payable invoice. At the completion of my assignment I expect to have recovered lost cash within your systems for you to reinvest in your business as profits. In addition, I'll issue you a report offering recommendations to close systems gaps that are exposed as a result of my work. My fee will be a percentage of the money I bring back for you. Whatever we can agree on."

The plan did indeed capture his interest. There was nothing to lose and everything to gain. But understandably, he needed more background. He was a cautious, conservative man, which is partly why he was president of an industrial corporation.

In the next half-hour we had one of the most memorable discussions I've experienced in business.

Our discussion led to the development of my program and how far into his business my research would take me. It was no easy task to explain how something as apparently trivial as a sales invoice, a freight ticket, or a pallet on a factory floor could turn into a $100,000 profit savings.

When a consultant finds in a review that a vendor overcharges for a product, the client is entitled to a cash refund adjustment. On the other hand, if a client charges less than the agreed price on a sales invoice, or makes an operations error, or receives no credit memo for returns—these are all functional areas where the client can recover cash lost through operational transactions. There must be a hundred ways—from computer errors to contract disputes—in which a business organization can lose cash.

This explanation must have had all the ingredients Mr. Liebman needed to make his decision. "Mr. Sinn," he said, "I want you to talk to my financial vice-president and controller. Today, if you can. I think we can use your program here."

And so I began my career as a management consultant.

Development of the COM System

Like any other business service, a quality product, a sincere approach, and reliable service (work) will make a management consultant firm successful. The cash operations management consultant service has weathered the tests of time. Many industrial and commercial organizations have reaped benefits both in increases in the percentage of profits and in systems and procedures improvements by following the important concepts of this program.

In time, the program developed an expanded philosophy in its approach to identifying methods for improving cash profits. New Ideas emerged from successful cases, which opened avenues of valuable profit sources for the business organization in every departmental function. Eventually these new areas introduced keys to a cash operations management system, which revealed unique methods on how companies could improve cash profits in every part of their organizations. The accomplishments in the COM system were organized patterns of business improvement that attracted business operations management people. The unique part of the system is that it highlights cash-profit functions in the operations part of a business, which supersedes the view that accountants guard profit dollars in this area.

Elements of the COM System

The important elements of the cash operations management system can be expanded into improved values of operational processing costs, strategies of operations analysis in purchasing, marketing, production, and accounting, as well as the introduction of new profit principles through cash evaluation, inventory controls, and processing. This system is a profit revelation designed to detect functional cash problems in every part of an industrial or commercial business organization. Billions of business dollars, it has been established, are lost annually through cash-operational areas.

The flow of the cash operations management system through the business organization is shown in Figure 2.1. The mechanics of the system and the reason for its emerging on today's business scene is explained further in the next chapter. In the succeeding chapters we follow how all parts of the business organization adapt to the elements of the COM system illustrated in this flowchart.

Figure 2.1 Cash operations management system

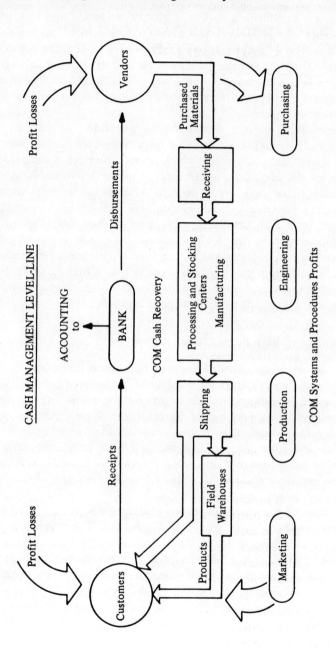

3. Cash Operations Management: Where Cash Operations Profits Are Found

Which employees in a business organization are directly responsible for assuring the company president that all of the company's dollars have been accounted for and spent accurately and properly? Is it the marketing employees? Through billing and shipping, the marketing department touches most of the dollars that flow through the organization. Is it Purchasing? This is the second largest area. It processes at least 50 percent of the sales dollars through the organization's complex business system. Is it the EDP systems people? Electronic data processing controls the systems and has access to information on sales, purchases, inventory statistics, and forecasts for the company. Or perhaps it's Accounting. The other departments think it is. If it isn't, what other department could it be? No physical dollars flow through the accounting department or the general ledger—only paperwork.

Who, then, *is* responsible for the company's money? The answer is: *none of the above.* The company's money is controlled according to systems and procedures within the company. How well the money is controlled depends on how well the various departments operate and control these systems and procedures.

In this book, however, we introduce an isolated business principle that will supplement yet bypass systems and procedures controls to achieve additional profits for the organization. It is an approach that will go directly to profit dollars (100-percent profit dollars) for an immediate review of how the business organization is handling its money.

The principle is *cash operations management.* It is a successful cash management approach that is used to review the basic operational elements of the business as they affect cash management in the form of billing, disbursements, returns, shipping, receiving, and so forth. It probes areas of the business that do not show up on the surface in financial statements or on weekly reports. It is the growth of a business idea that has a dual purpose: (1) the impact of *cash recovery* for profits, and (2) systems and procedures *profit improvement opportunities.*

How Do We Find Additional Cash Profits?

Now that the term "cash profits" has been mentioned a couple of times, let us delve into the basic, important question: How do we find additional cash profits in the business organization? What values are received by applying cash operations management skills? Additional cash profits are found by conducting a cash operations management program *below the cash management level-line.*

When cash dollars escape the control of a company's systems and procedures, they drop through the systems into an area below, an area in the business organization that I have identified as the *physical dollars* part of the business, below the cash-management level-line (CMLL). This is where you will find actual products in inventories, purchased raw materials, operations problems in shipping and receipts, and returns of materials, backorders or overorders. It is an area just beyond the reach of employees in the company unless employees and management make a concentrated effort to reach out for it. But very few managers do.

The cash management level-line is the division line where actual physical dollars are divided from dollars coded in accounting. Accounting-coded dollars represent only those dollars on financial statements (via the general ledger); physical dollars are the dollars subject to loss or gain that are controlled by business-operations functions within an organization.

Physical dollars are materials and services distributed throughout the business spectrum. This is *money.* If you lose account of or waste this money, or ignore functional activities controlling these materials or services, then you are losing cash profits—below the cash management level-line.

A business organization simply cannot ignore these losses and still expect to meet its financial obligations in the company. Someone in the organization must convince the company president that the dollars that potentially can escape are being controlled by good systems, good procedures, and good audits. If these dollars are not soon controlled, serious consideration must be given to the cash operations management principles introduced in this book.

Figure 3.1 adds another dimension to the structure of cash operations management in the business organization.

Why Are These CMLL Dollars Important?

Why should you bother to go after the dollars lost below the cash management level-line? There are two important reasons why profit-minded management people should adopt additional profit incentives in the cash operations management area of the business organization:

Figure 3.1   Profit control through cash operations management

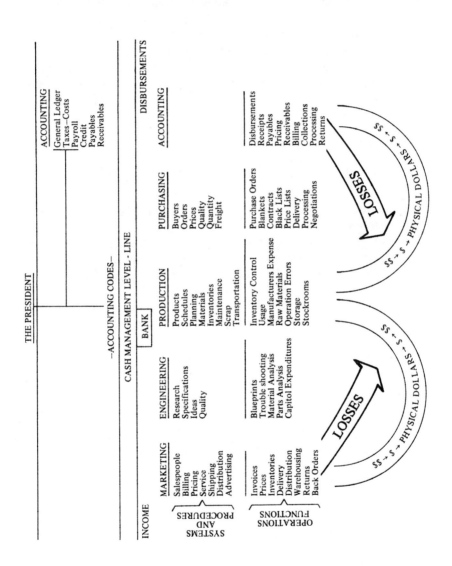

(1) This is an expansive, dominant area for business profits, which has been neglected by management people. As we noted in Figure 2.1, every productive department in the organization (not to exclude Personnel, which wasn't shown) plays an effective role in making profits through COM. Total dollars flowing through the company pass by way of cash operations management. This includes billing, disbursements, shipping products, and receiving raw materials, as well as all the functional problems, disasters, errors, oversights, laziness, and so on that can cause a company to lose cash. This total profit spectrum represents your company's cash position—*below the CMLL.*

(2) These dollars are *100-percent profit dollars.* In our search for profits in cash operations management, we look for 100-percent profit dollars. What are 100-percent profit dollars? Let us look at an example that should explain the difference between the 100-percent profit dollar and the regular business profit dollar. When a customer changes his or her mind and returns a thousand dollars worth of sales, the loss is likely to be only a 5-percent profit loss (whatever margin of profit the company realizes). When a purchasing agent makes an error in buying a thousand-dollar shipment of unreturnable goods, however, this purchase means the complete loss of the business transaction—$1,000 in profits, or *100-percent dollars.* To simplify: $100 saved in purchases means $100 added to gross profit, *whereas* $100 in additional sales adds perhaps only $5 to gross profits.

This brings up an ever-perplexing question regarding decision making in business management. On one hand, management will spend hundreds of thousands of dollars in sales administrative costs, expenses, leased automobiles, and fringe benefits to bring in 5-percent profit dollars. On the other hand, most companies will not spend a dime on employees or outside help to capture and maintain profits of 100-percent dollars. The following chapters will disclose some high-profit examples of how costly this business practice can be to a company.

Where Do We Look for CMLL Dollars?

New profits are usually always welcome in a business organization. If there is a good method for increasing profits in a business, most business people grasp at the idea. This book is written to provide just such an idea. Now, where do we take our first step to recover hidden dollars?

A good example is to compare the moves made by oil companies in recent years—after the gasoline shortage (or hoax) of 1974—with the opportunities opened to your own company during the same period.

Before the "price freeze of 1973," oil companies stopped drilling on a productive well when costs surpassed the income potential. This means that when gasoline was 35¢ a gallon at the pumps, the oil companies drilled to the point of their markup of profit; *but there was still more oil in that well.* To dig it out, however, required sinking more dollars in the hole.

So what happened? Overnight, it seemed, gasoline prices went out of sight. Now the oil companies were promised more profits, more dollars, to *dig deeper into the hole,* because twice the profit value was promised to them for the additional oil left in the hole.

The same enterprising offer was made to every business organization in the United States. The same principle applies in your own company. You, too, have experienced increases of 200 to 300 percent in the value of the materials and products that have flowed through your company since 1974. Now you also have the opportunity to reopen an "oil well of profits" for your company.

Like most others, your company experienced losses or discrepancies in its cash controls and systems prior to 1974. Now these systems and control problems have grown. Losses have probably doubled and tripled if improved controls have not been implemented, or your working staff beefed up. Those ignored profits now lie in old files in your company, waiting to be recaptured—in *100 percent profit dollars.* Would you ever need a better situation in which to begin a COM profit program?

In retrospect, the foundation of a good COM profit system lies in the back files of your company's cash records. These files include billing and disbursements records, correspondence and pricing information from both areas, and other transactions, notes, and memos pertaining to this subject.

Once an analysis is made of these areas, cash operational problems will promptly come to the fore in the form of increased profits. From there, channels of opportunity will take the analysis expert to every department in the company.

My case histories in the following chapters describe various profit situations that, it is hoped, will furnish answers to your own business problems and profit possibilities.

While reading through these pages of case histories of profits, you should keep in mind making a decision regarding your own company. It is important for you to decide who in your organization can best conduct a "profit program" for your company. Perhaps you the reader are the most likely prospect, since your interest in cash profits has taken you this far.

My recommendation is that you put this book into the hands of someone in your company who can make the decision to acquire more cash profits. Then tell that person you are interested in becoming the cash-profit expert in your company. In a short time I guarantee you will be recognized as *the* profit person of your company.

How Much Can Be Realized Through CMLL Profit Dollars?

Cash operations management losses occur in every part of a business organization and in all types of organizations—industrial, service, distribution, and financial. Not even government organizations are immune to them. The question is, What return will be diverted from work applied to 100-percent profit dollars in a COM system?

There is no set pattern. Companies benefiting from this program have been of all sizes and sell all types of products and services. Cash recovery has come as abundantly from companies with sales of $10 million as from those with sales of $100 million. Systems and procedures profit improvements have experienced increases as high as 50 percent. They will consistently add a percentage point or two or more in profits to the percentage of sales.

What more could be asked of a program? There is absolutely no cost involved in conducting the project. Cash recovery pays for all analysis hours, expenses, or costs consumed, and could conceivably contribute another million dollars *in cash* to your company bank account.

As we note in subsequent chapters, it is not unreasonable to expect a multimillion dollar return in systems and procedures profit from the COM Program—all of which will be acquired by using cash operations management skills.

This program is not complex. Throughout, it should be rated as a primary source for subsidizing profits in your business. A skeleton crew or even one person (because we go after 100-percent profit dollars) could produce as much in profits as 1,000 employees. Your most expensive people, vice-presidents and top managers, could sit in on meetings week after week, month after month, and still not accomplish the new profit output that 2,000 hours of a COM program could. There are reasons for this, which will come out in later chapters, having to do with employee responsibilities and allocation of time.

Throughout the years of building this COM system, I have constantly searched for meaningful information and statistics that will identify this program as an *overall* business approach to new profits. My years of experience now tell me without reservation that additional profits can be contributed by every department in the business organization.

The first case history from my consultant's file is presented in the following chapter for this very purpose. It illustrates vividly that cash operations management can be a universal company problem.

4. Testers, Profits, and Dollars: Cash Operations Management Throughout the Organization

Early one morning, while shuffling through the large accounting department of the Cosmic Corporation, I stepped on a sheet of paper lying next to a payables desk. Reaching down to pick it up, I noticed that it was a Xerox copy of a six-month-old invoice. I glanced at the amount column on the face of the invoice. My heart sank when I read the amount: $12,600.

The disregard for high-value dollars in companies causes me mental anguish at times. Here was an old $12,600 invoice tainted with such neglect that a total stranger from outside the company (a consultant) was mistakenly given the privilege of grinding it into the carpet. What was the story behind it?

I immediately stopped and turned to the accounts-payable clerk.

"Has this invoice been paid?" I asked, handing it to him.

"I can tell you if anything was received on it, but you'll have to go over to cash disbursements to determine if it has been paid," the clerk replied.

"Fine," I said. "Has the material been received?" He checked his open receipts file and his purchase order file.

"Nope, nothing on it." After six months, this was to be expected.

My stop at cash disbursements revealed that no payment had been made. The vendor had sent the additional copy of the invoice, asking for payment.

I was overcome with curiosity by this time. I had no intention of sidestepping a $12,600 expenditure. My next move would be to check purchasing.

Again, dismay. The people in Purchasing had absolutely no written information on this product or invoice; nor could they find an open order from the subject vendor. As a matter of fact, they didn't even recognize the product—which wasn't unexpected; this vendor had sold the client more than 500 different products.

We also found that the part number listed on the invoice was erroneous. At this point it seemed we might be on a case of fraud. The purchasing department had no way of identifying the contents on the $12,600 invoice.

Where did this leave me, the consultant? In the hallway, to be sure, but pointed in the direction of the receiving department and the stockroom.

The receiving clerk did not recognize the product. The stockroom clerk simply said that the product was not in his "cage."

Now the problem became more complex. The basic procedures and systems for purchasing a product were not functioning. The time had come for the consultant to use his imagination. There must be something on the invoice that would lead to an answer.

We will call the product a soil tester. That was the description on the invoice. It was designed to test samples of soil at construction sites for long-range durability before construction of a building or bridge at the site. A good idea.

After searching the invoice painstakingly, I did turn up something—a sales tax. There was $600 in sales tax charged on the invoice. This indicated capital expenditure, meaning that the engineers might be using the product in the company's testing laboratories. At a quantity of 100, however, this wasn't likely. Nevertheless, my next stop was at the office of the vice-president of engineering, where I presented my problem.

"No way could we use a hundred soil testers," the top engineer replied. "But you might check back in production. They're making asphalt-consistency testers for construction—up front at the south end of the plant."

This at least was a lead, better than anyone had given me yet. When I reached the production department, I approached the assistant production manager in charge.

"No, we have nothing to do with soil testers," he yelled over the noise of the machines. "We only make the asphalt testers. But you know where you should try? You should ask someone in the marketing and advertising department. They buy soil testers for an advertising product."

Can you imagine that? I thanked him and left. What kind of cash-operations problem had I taken on here? My search had begun in the disbursements end of the company and led all the way to the receiving dock. Now I'm supposed to find the answer to a purchased no-name product worth $12,600 all the way at the other end of the company, in the marketing and advertising department. Is it any wonder that dollars get lost in a business organization? It seemed that systems and procedures just are not designed to control this kind of thing.

Let us review where I had been up to this point. The following areas had been investigated:

1. Accounts-payable department
2. Cash disbursements area
3. Purchasing department
4. Receiving department (dock)

5. Stockroom
6. Engineering department
7. Production department

My search had taken me to seven functional departments, and I had interviewed numerous employees. More than three quarters of the company had been reviewed, and not one employee had been found who was remotely connected or interested in $12,600 worth of products that their company president had been obliged to buy with cash dollars.

My next move was to interview people in Marketing and Advertising to determine if they were responsible for the purchase of the soil testers. After talking to a couple of sales and advertising executives I was sent to a national sales service manager. Here my search ended. But the discovery of a cash-operations-management nightmare was on the verge of lift-off.

Final Step of the Interviews

"Yes, Jerry," John Teagarten said, "I'm the one who purchased those testers. We've bought over 1,000 now, plus another 1,000 that are in the plans. And Purchasing does have a purchase order on them. I gave it to them myself."

Could you imagine—this long search, and now I had found someone with answers. I was elated. My questions were put to him in rapid succession: Why don't other employees know about these products? Who has responsibility for receiving these testers? Where are the testers located now? Are they being sold? Who's shipping them to the customer? "Fill me in, John," I pleaded. "Do you really owe $12,600 to this vendor for the products listed on the invoice?"

"Yes, we do," John replied. This guy was astute. He was one of the best I've seen in industrial customer service. "But it's not as simple as it may appear," he explained. "I'm having problems getting other departments to participate in this project." He explained further by saying: "It's important to understand that this is an advertising-promotion program. Our company decal is displayed on these testers. It's really a break-even product. We don't expect to make much profit. Marketing wants the program in every way, and it's successful. We can't get enough of those testers. But for some reason it's become an ostrich. Purchasing and Accounting have not particularly opposed the program, but they haven't jumped at it either."

What John had told me in a thorough, extended interview was that there was a major systems and procedure problem in cash operations management. It was a unique business problem because it involved every part of the organization. And that is my reason for bringing it up at this time, in the early part of this book. It's an excellent example of problems that can occur in COM throughout an entire organization.

First, there was already a cash recovery probability here. Since this product is resold to a customer, as John Teagarten had mentioned, why should a sales tax be charged? This was a use tax, and my client was not using the product. Second, this invoice came off the vendor's computer; therefore, apparently, a sales tax had been written into the vendor's EDP program and was consistently charging a tax on the total 1,000 testers billed. Perhaps cash recovery was $6,000. We would find out. It was time to get the Com program underway again. We would take it step by step.

Testors Program Errors in the COM System

The reasons why I had trouble locating the tester product at the Cosmic Corporation were myriad. The problem, however, began when normal business *systems* and *procedures* were bypassed.

Apparently, one day the departmental vice-presidents at Cosmic got together and agreed to try the tester product in an advertising program but only on a temporary basis. After the agreement no good thinking went into how the company would manage or control the dollar investment involved. One thing, however, was decided on; since the tester would be used only temporarily, *no part number* would be assigned the product; accounting would merely pick it up as a miscellaneous income expense entry. This was a mistake. This company could not afford to make such a decision. All you managers who might be thinking of making a similar decision for your company, please read on.

Let's break the problem down by department and function. After I explain the contents and effects of the cash operations system, I will conclude with recommendations and an explanation of actions taken.

Purchasing

The testers had been drop shipped from a manufacturer in Los Angeles. This meant they were shipped by the manufacturer (Company B) directly to my client in Chicago but were billed through my client's vendor (Company A).

The purchase order was written to Company A, but the material was shipped from Los Angeles under company B's name and purchase order number (Company A's drop shipment purchase order number). Thus, when the material arrived at John Teagarten's plant, there was no reference to his purchase order number. Only Company A's purchase order number to the drop shipper (Company B) was shown on the shipping papers. The result was Purchasing's disenchantment with the prospect of attempting to control receipts of the testers.

Another notable point here is that the reason why I could not find a purchase order in Purchasing or Accounts Payable was that the order was filed in the closed file. Why? Because the initial 500 testers were all that were listed on the second page of the purchase order. The second 500 were ordered as a condition of selling the first 500. Thus, when 500 were shown as received, both the purchasing and accounts payable departments closed their orders. This was another mistake. Both should have read the face of the purchase order—page one—not only for notation of quantities but for information content. On top of all this, price also turned out to be a significant factor.

Cost Accounting

Because this product was to be only a temporary advertising program, the cost accountants were told to book the testers through a special miscellaneous income expense account in the general ledger. This released the accountants from originating a "part number," which obviously caused the product to escape inventory control. Why the accountants' management would want to do this is beyond me. It escapes all good business principles of product control. But it happened.

The reason it happened was this. Verbal communication got in the way of "paperwork analysis dollars." If the accountants, or vice-presidents, had multiplied the figures on the purchase order (1,000 testers purchased at $120 each, plus $30 for handling, plus $135 sales price), they would have realized a $285,000 cash transaction that would certainly have warranted inventory control. Values, among other important features, must always be a determining factor when controlling an inventory product through business operations. In addition, analysis and thought are requirements in high-value decisions. This project should not have been seen as just another small advertising promotion.

Another significant element here is that the Cosmic Corporation carried products in its inventory that had less than $200 movement per year. Why would they ignore a $285,000 product, which has the potential of turning twice?

This is an authentic example of an operations problem that will happen in companies, and it should offer that much more importance to the value of cash operations management. A predominant cash problem was about to fall through the systems—below the CMLL.

Electronic Data Processing

The special miscellaneous income expense account established for these testers bypassed the regular billing system normally used for items with inventory control part numbers. The use of special invoices through EDP was the only method available for billing the soil tester customers, which is where a major cash problem occurred: the special invoice EDP program had some bugs in it.

Invoicing and Billing   The deficiencies in the EDP special billing program were not minor ones. Here is a description of the relevant loopholes in the program: (1) occasionally certain tester shipments were not billed; (2) in other instances, only partial shipments were billed; (3) at times, only freight charges were billed, but the material shipped was omitted from the billing amount. This was a significant cash operations systems problem, since a large volume of sales, in addition to testers, was channeled through the company's special invoicing process.

Receiving Department   The stockroom clerk accepted only the parts that had inventory control numbers. Therefore the receiving clerk could not deliver the soil testers to the stockroom. Inevitably, this $285 cash product was exposed to eager hands in sealed boxes that could easily be sold on the outside (security).

In addition, there was no purchase order in the receiving file to match the shipper's name (Company B)—a systems deficiency. Purchasing, or John Teagarten in Marketing, should have established a cross-reference on the purchase order for departmental identification purposes. But Purchasing hadn't even known about the drop-shipper. Teagarten, in Marketing, had handled this purchase.

Shipping Department   Shipping clerks pulled tester products from the receiving department floor, for palletizing and sending to their six outside plants. This evaded inventory control procedures a second time. The company's plants used the identical inventory control system; thus the products were exposed again, on a national scale, on floors outside stockrooms in six cities across the United States—important ones in Atlanta, Dallas, and Los Angeles, where both manufacturing plants and distribution centers were located.

These shipments triggered intercompany billing to plant accounts. Individual bills of lading and handwritten invoices were used as shipping documents. No perpetual inventory record was kept to verify that the testers had been received or shipped. In some instances, the only proof of receipt from the vendor was the proof-of-shipment papers to an outside plant. Let me emphasize again that this was a $285 cash transaction product. The controls on it were so flimsy that it was hard to believe that experienced business people were overseeing the project.

Inventory Control   No business record on the testers was kept on the location of products at any particular period of time. The miscellaneous income expense account entry only verified vendor invoices paid and shipments billed (in/out). The company was not expecting much in profits (nor in losses) from the "advertising promotion"; so little attention was paid, or importance attached to, the overall movement in general ledger account number 742, the tester's account.

Because no inventory control number had been assigned to the product, the stockroom people would not admit the product into their "cage" (according to systems and procedures). That's why no perpetual inventory record was kept on the product. Systems and procedures could not bend to accommodate a $285,000 cash operations transaction.

Usage   Despite the restrictive problems that accompanied this product, the soil tester was a hot sales item. The price was low (the tester was sold at a loss), which made it a good buy, and John Teagarten could not get enough of them. When the consultant ran a physical inventory, however, 45 units had been sitting in the Texas plant for more than four months, and no one in the other plants knew of their existence. In addition to other problems, there was obviously a communications systems problem in identifying relief of inventory through sales statistics. The sales coordinator back at corporate headquarters (a marketing services clerk) thought the inventory had been deplenished to zero.

Freight Costs and Handling   The testers were drop shipped from the manufacturer in Los Angeles directly to Chicago. My client in Chicago divided the quantities, then promptly shipped them to their plants. Strange as it may seem, some of the units were shipped right back to the plant in Los Angeles, while others went back to Texas. This was a duplication of freight costs at the rate of $30 per unit one way. Again, cash operations management was ignored; a poor purchase and inventory control plan was employed. These were losses of profits—below the CMLL.

Returns and Allowances   No systems procedure was initiated for returning reject units to the manufacturer. It was understood that a new unit would be sent to the customer to replace the reject, but credit forms and follow-up procedures—from the corporate billing office to the manufacturer—were never established. A 10-percent return rate was reported from one plant but not verified. Since there was no control over the count of units sold and returned, the return rate could not be established.

The end result: (1) new units were shipped at no charge, and (2) reject units, still highly redeemable, were mislaid at one of several places (they could still have been in the customer's hands, in my client's plants, or buried at corporate headquarters, the distributor's warehouse, or the manufacturer).

Lost units and additional handling costs became a prominent factor in the overall cash operations problem.

List of Departments and Functions Included in COM Review

Now let us update the list of departments and functions we have reviewed, to determine how complex this cash operations management problem is. When that is complete, we will run a systems analysis on the problems and discrepancies to determine the extent of profit loss. We will also include a synopsis of how each department could have corrected its operations and avoided contributing to the problem.

List of Departments and Functions in COM Profit and Loss

---

accounts payable	cost accounting
cash disbursements	general accounting
purchasing	EDP
receiving	inventory control
stockroom	security
engineering	shipping
production	outside plants—receiving
sales and marketing	outside plants—shipping
advertising	outside plants—billing
sales service	outside plants—inventory control
sales promotion	intercompany accounting
billing	transportation

Two dozen corporate departments and critical functional business areas were affected in this, so it must be considered a costly cash operations management problem in the company. Now let us find out just how costly this type problem can become and determine where procedures went wrong.

Consultant's Systems Analysis of Tester Losses

First, an invoice for $12,000 and a similar value in tangible products should never be difficult to trace through a business system. The lack of interest in financial judgment was abundantly evident. Employees were apparently so secure in their jobs that they could ignore accomplishment and profit incentives. Under such circumstances, the business organization pays a high price.

Now let us analyze the systems in the departments on the above list and describe the discrepancies in functions, as well as the cash-profit losses. We will take it department by department.

Accounts Payable/Cash Disbursements/Purchasing

A significant cash-profit problem resulted from the origin of the purchase order. The national sales service manager wrote up the purchase order for the tester. But this was a purchasing agent's job. Some significant points are bound to be overlooked when sales people attempt to handle purchasing people's work, or vice versa. Here are the major profit points that were overlooked in this case:

1. The quantity of the purchase was misunderstood by Payables and by Purchasing. Both departments had their purchase orders closed (complete) after the first 500 units were delivered. The second 500 units were written up on additional pages of the purchase orders, along with pertinent price information. Technically, the sales people had all the pertinent information on the purchase order; but the key factors of quantity and price were assigned secondary importance and placed on the back pages.

2. Payables and purchasing lost price and quantity information on closed purchase orders. Payables had no reference for incoming invoices, for prices, or for receiving information. When shipping and receiving tickets came from the drop shipper, there was no matching paperwork. In time the purchase orders were discarded, with the result that old, $12,600 unpaid invoices turned up needing a lot of costly legwork to qualify for payment.

3. The people in Payables did not get the price message on the testers. The vendor was to charge $120 per unit for the first 500 units. If my client needed the second 500, the price was to drop to $115 each for all units. The payables clerks accepted the first 500 at $120 each (billed amount) and did not apply for a credit memo when the second 500 were shipped. In fact, *no* company employee took an interest in the responsibility for collecting the overcharge of $5 per unit. The total cash loss on the first 500 was $2,500.

COM

This purchase situation is a significant example of profit and loss in cash operations management in business organizations. This is the "special purchase" on special, out-of-the-ordinary, purchase terms. The same applies to special sales terms. Some companies freely mark up special sales items as much as 450 percent, and perhaps more. It is piracy, but purchasing agents and management will be stuck with it if they do not shop around or plan their purchases with sufficient lead time.

The purchase agreement on the above purchase order was written with anticipation that the payables clerk or the purchase clerk would vary from his or her systemized paths, that of routine work habits. The clerk was expected to stop in the middle of the purchase order deliveries to make a decision by informing management to change the price of the testers to $115 per unit.

This, however, would involve originating a debit memo to bill the vendor for the additional $5 per unit ($120 to $115 per unit)—a total of $2,500. (If the vendor was not up-to-date on this special agreement, then the vendor could be expected to give the clerk trouble on the debit memo—which is exactly what happened in this case. Even a responsible clerk cannot be expected to handle this type of maneuvering and still keep up with the pressure of paperwork from unsympathetic managers. Numerous clerical and supervisory functions must be performed to make adjustments on special items.

In most business organizations this is entirely too much to expect from a clerk. It is not an intelligence issue, it is a work-habit issue and a volume-of-paperwork issue. When clerical people stop their paperwork function to handle a special task, they are neglecting their primary responsibility: to move paperwork through the department. When paperwork backs up, their supervisors use this as a criterion for nonproduction. Thus a negative element enters into the business-profits picture. The end result is that clerks produce only paperwork, because only *reprimand will result from doing profit-oriented tasks.*

This is where CASH OPERATIONS MANAGEMENT finds its place in the business organization. This work is too much of a burden for clerical people. Somewhere, someone considers this work beneath the plateau of managers. The end result is that profit work does not get done. This is a shameful conclusion, but such a negative, narrow-minded approach governs most company office procedures. An honest attempt to hire another employee to share the work load of the more experienced clerk, in order to free that clerk to make some profit decisions, would pay big dividends. In this case, following up on the tester prices would have saved the company thousands of dollars in profits, as we will see.

4. Something different happened on the second shipment of 500 testers. Instead of an overcharge of $5 per unit, the bottom fell out on the price of the vendor's computer; the overcharge became an additional $48 per unit. The vendor's computer went off special prices and regular bluebook prices were charged. Vendor's advantage (VA) was exercised here, a subject we will study in another chapter. The additional charges, however, were issued and *paid*. This was total negligence on the part of Payables (a result of personnel turnover), as well as lack of supervision on the part of accounting management. The payment system for the testers had failed completely at this stage. The unrealistic overcharge of $48 per unit on the second 500 totaled an enormous profit loss of $24,200.

5. A state sales tax of 5 percent was charged on the invoice. A sales tax is a use tax. The regulations read that only the user of a product must pay the tax. The testers were not used by my client. Rather, they were used by my client's customers. My client did not have to pay the tax. Thus Payables missed it, probably because they thought Engineering used the testers *and* because the vendor charged the tax. (They operated on the premise that the vendor is right, a costly practice in business.) Whatever the reason, perhaps total negligence, the additional sales tax cost this company $7,200 in cash profits—below the cash management level-line.

A synopsis of cash operations management profit losses for the initial three departments—payables, cash disbursements, and purchasing—reveals a good beginning to an effective COM program:

COM Program Statistics

Cash recovery	*Amount*
price: $5 per unit	$2,500
price: $48 per unit	24,200
sales tax	7,200
total recovery	$33,900

Systems and procedures benefits:
detection of poor price control

Systems Improvement Ideas

1. Purchasing should originate all purchase orders. Other departments are good at their own work.
2. Free up clerks to make profit decisions and to meet their paperwork responsibilities. This is not to relieve supervisors; its purpose is to

    make more employees more aware of making profits for the company.

3. Educate payables clerks in the basics of payment on special purchases.
4. Educate payables people in the payment of sales taxes.
5. Educate payables and purchasing people never to assume the vendor's invoice price is correct. The purchaser's correct price on the product will be on special or regular price lists, on correspondence, or on contracts. *It will not be on the vendor's invoice.*

Receiving/Stockroom/Inventory Control/Security

If there is no inventory control on business products, there is bound to be profit loss. Employees will do the work they are assigned, but if their job is made more difficult they will likely refuse extra project responsibility. "It's not my job," the saying goes. This conjecture applies to inventory control as much or perhaps more than to any other area of the business organization.

In the testers project, the stockroom people would not allow the receiving department to store the products in the stockroom because of the lack of an inventory control number. (This was also true of six outside plants.) Inevitably, the receiving clerk did not want to argue with the stockroom clerk; thus the testers were stored inside, in the receiving area next to the dock.

The exposed product was boxed and ready to be carried out the side door by any adept thief looking for this kind of thing. In my analysis of the first testers, which was an enormous task, the testers were being shipped throughout the country; 44 units were missing, beyond paperwork control.

The total neglect, in terms of dollars in lost units for the 1,000 units, was $24,200. Prior to my work, it appeared that no employee had any intention of accounting for the lost units. After my review, John Teagarten, in Marketing, investigated the lost units for recovery, but Accounting was not interested in the lost dollars.

All outward appearances led me to believe there was an interdepartmental conflict here. Each department seemed to want to "hang one" on another department. The cost of this practice—internal corporate entanglements—can be incredible. Just in this inventory control area alone, the profit-loss dollars amounted to $24,200, a major portion of which was redeemable in cash recovery. John Teagarten recovered many of these units after the review, from customers as well as salespeople who use them as sales samples. (Salespeople were selling their samples without reporting the sale.) Others were recovered as rejects.

COM Program Statistics

Cash Recovery	Amount
Lost units recovered	$18,200
Systems and Procedures Benefits:	
Lost units not recovered	6,000
Total profit dollars	$24,200

Systems Improvement Ideas

1. Always use an inventory control system for all business products flowing through the organization. If the product cannot fit into your regular mechanized systems, use a manual system. The product control manual described in a later chapter offers a guide in this area.
2. Special products or special purchases should never become involved in departmental conflicts. Concentrated functional work procedures (interest) should be applied to special transactions in business. Anticipate the loopholes in the system, then close them before the start of the program. This takes little effort, and will save much in the way of profit dollars.
3. Never tempt industrial thieves with finished, boxed products. People have numerous reasons for stealing business products. Good security precautions can minimize some temptations and losses.
4. Develop an incentive for employees to make and think *profits* in your company. Try to overcome interdepartmental profit conflicts.

Sales/Advertising/Billing/EDP

Selling the tester product was no problem, perhaps because it was a good product; but then, the price as an advertising product was right too. The problem was billing for the tester. My analysis revealed that, of the first 500 units shipped, 23 simply were not billed to the customer. Outside plant shipments to customers were escaping the computer invoice printing.

Although the EDP system was the primary cause, an accounting or marketing audit analysis should have identified the problem.

COM Note

The most important contribution in the above example was the discovery of the systems-billing problem. This problem wasn't confined to the testers; there must have been $7 million dollars annual volume channeled through special billing at this company. A five-percent invoicing dropout (shipped but not billed) would amount to approximately $300,000 dollars in profit loss at the above volume. This is an incredible loss for a secondary-area billing function in any business organization.

The statistics given above on the billing-systems error for the total 1,000 units registered a cash profit loss of $13,110 (46 units at $285 each). This was eventually rebilled, for a total cash recovery of the lost money by using COM program techniques.

COM Program Statistics:

Cash Recovery	*Amount*
Did not invoice customer	$13,110

Systems and Procedures Benefits:
   corporate systems computer program
   problem possibility in billing

special invoices	$300,000 (est.)

Systems Improvement Ideas

1. If a new system is so complicated that in-house employees cannot recognize a problem, then management should get outside assistance in reviewing a system.
2. Intercompany systems and audit-analysis procedures must be included in every organization's systems. Do not make the mistake of thinking that departmental employees will perform without error. Employees are often burdened with responsibilities. The company law-of-responsibility rule (see Chapter 12) says that if employees appear to be out of paperwork, management will tie them down with more responsibilities. This eliminates "think time" for profits.

Shipping/Transportation/Usage

Approximately 24 percent of the testers produced in Los Angeles were shipped to Chicago, then back to my client's warehouses in Los Angeles and Dallas. The duplication of freight charges on the total 1,000-unit package, at $30 per unit, amounted to $7,200 one way, plus shipments back in my client's own trucks (240 units). No cash recovery was applicable; this was a permanent loss.

This transportation function was handled by Jim Freman, the corporate office sales service manager. Jim was responsible for supplying the plants with the product, for inventory control, for usage by the plant, and for originating the shipping papers that would trigger both intercompany and billing to customers. Everything was done on a manual basis.

He did a reasonably good job, considering the systems, forms, and procedures available to assist him in the work. But overall, losses to the total system were feeding on the weaknesses of this shipping area.

Product usage must not have been considered important in the testers program. The vice-presidents apparently did not anticipate much sales volume on the product. Perhaps they were concentrating on the unit count. It was learned, however, that value should have been the key control issue on the testers, not the number of units.

A physical inventory that I conducted indicated that 45 units were shipped to and held at the Texas warehouse for a period of four to six months. In the meantime, the other plants scrimped for units to sell to waiting customers.

This obvious usage problem pulled $12,825 out of cash circulation for that period, which stole dollars from cash profits. The amount of profits were: (1) $513 interest at 12% on sales dollars uncollected, and (2) $324 interest in paid cash on purchase dollars. Product usage can steal cash from the organization in numerous ways. The example given above was the least costly in cash profits on the testers program; but that is not always the case, as we will see in the next chapter.

COM Program Statistics

Cash Recovery	*Amount*
	None
Systems and Procedures Benefits:	
Freight cost duplication	$7,200
Usage Interest Loss	837
Total profit dollars	$8,037

Systems Improvement Ideas

1. The transportation, freight, and shipping areas of an industrial or a commercial organization are notable cash profit areas that require watching closely by management. Freight details such as rates, processing costs, duplicate charges, reversed charges on terms, and indirect routes costs can cost your company plenty. And these details did not even touch the $7,200 lost in the systems problem described above. The subject of profits on freight costs must be concentrated in a good systems profit cycle in every business organization.

2. The lack of usage systems control can multiply cash profit losses into excessive amounts. Inventory shelf costs are high, as are purchase investment costs. This fact is discussed more fully below; the case described above, however, is an excellent example of how additional cash can be lost in an overall usage systems problem.

Returns and Allowances

Reject tester units could not be accounted for in my review. It was understood, though, that they were included in the 88 missing units, worth $24,200.

Four units, however, were returned to the vendor without credit and never heard from again; the vendor simply could not locate them. This was a familiar comment on the subject of tester returns. Cash recovery on the above loss was $1,100. My client proved shipment.

What is important here is that the return system for rejected testers was a dismal failure. New replacement testers were sent to the customers, but they were under no strict obligation to return them. All costs incurred in returns were absorbed by my client, and all returns came back C.O.D. The customer could not lose. On the other hand, my client should not have lost either. The peculiar part was that no employee in my client's company knew of the losses on returns or attempted to prevent dollar losses of reject testers; marketing merely continued to send replacements.

COM Program Statistics

Cash Recovery	*Amount*
proof of delivery on testers	$1,100

Systems and Procedures Benefits: submitted

Systems Improvement Ideas

Good follow-through on a sales program requires a well thought out return policy on reject units. This should be a flawless plan that will give the seller complete control and knowledge of the location of the product. If weaknesses show up in a special sales program, it is natural to assume that there are weaknesses in the overall returns of company products. We can also assume that big cash profit amounts are involved in these losses.

A returns service center is a separate profit center. It is virtually a separate company with a dead-end product to merchandise. Its income resources are dependent on doing something to replenish the dead product. In a positive sense, with good business interest applied, it can be a flourishing business.

The problem in services occurs when the reject product does not reach the service center. If too many outlets return a reject product, paperwork becomes too cumbersome to control, and the reject ends up in the hands of people in the company who don't care about reject products. The result is a *cash loss*—a lost or destroyed $285 product that may have needed only a 35¢ part.

Good control of reject products requires a good control center for service. All rejects should be shipped to this control center and received, using a simple but well-planned repair service form. Complete directions on what action is to be taken—what is to be done to the product, where it is to be returned and charged, and so on—are the basic requirements for cash operations management of product returns.

Some top U.S. companies have good service centers. If your company is having problems in this area, my suggestion is that you look up one of these companies and ask to study their policies. They will probably feel complimented by your inquiry, which should meet with success.

Testers COM Program Benefits

Cash Recovery	Amount
price—$5 per unit	$2,500
price—$48 per unit	24,000
sales taxes	7,200
inventory control—lost units recovered	18,200
billing error—did not invoice customer	13,110*
tester returns saved	1,100
total cash recovery	$66,110
Systems and Procedure Losses	
inventory control—unrecovered lost units	$6,000
freight cost duplication	7,200
inventory usage—interest loss	837
total lost cash—future savings	$14,037
total losses on project before COM program	$80,147

*Estimated corporate loss: $300,000.

Recap on Cash Operations Management Benefits

What were the total benefits from applying cash operations management techniques to the testers advertising promotion in the above business organization? The answer is in two areas, cash recovery benefits and systems and procedures benefits—as described in Chapter 3.

The initial benefit was actual cash recovery. Lost cash dollars were returned to the client's bank account. We knew we had cash early in the review, as soon as we had facts on the sales tax charges. The $7,200 sales tax paid for all additional time warranted on the testers in the COM program. But much more cash was to come. First, price overcharges brought back $26,500 in debit memos, and billing errors were rebilled to the customers, for $13,110. Recovery of lost units and reject returns recovered $19,300, for a grand total in cash recovery of $66,110—a significant amount of cash in any business organization.

The total number of hours involved in the COM program in consultant and company employee time, was approximately 110. In the cash recovery area alone, the *profit return* to my client was at the rate of $600 an hour.

The other part of the cash program is the *unrecoverable* cash losses. These losses totaled $14,037. This equals 18 percent of total cash losses, which is extremely low compared to a total organization problem. This tester was a special program with simple systems and procedures; cash recovery was relatively easy. Generally, cash recovery is more difficult to achieve, and the percentage of unrecoverable cash is much more in value than in recoverable cash.

The important point here is knowing that the $14,037 was lost by a systems error, which can be corrected, as was the cash received. The $14,037 was lost—let that not be mistaken—no cash can be recovered on it. By correcting the system, however, the same loss should not occur the next year. This brings us to the primary reason for the cash operations management program: to acquire knowledge of systems errors so they can be corrected and profits can be earned in the future.

Testers Systems and Procedures COM Recommendations

What value can now be placed on the application of cash operations management in the testers program?

We know that profits can be increased through systems and procedures in the amount of $80,047. This much was realized through cash recovery and improved systems. Also, since sales are going so well, a price increase is applicable to cover the losses on the unit. An increase of $50 per unit would add $50,000 to cover hidden costs. In addition, it appears that a corporate billing systems error could reach an estimated $300,000 in cash losses. In accumulating all these dollars and ideas, we see that improving cash operations management was a valuable contribution to my client's company.

In retrospect, because the tester sales proved to be an extraordinary profit failure in terms of systems and procedures, you should assume that there are many other problems within the COM areas of this company. Although they will not be discussed in this book, that assumption is correct.

Major Systems and Procedures Recommendations

The major corporation systems areas in need of attention by my client, which were questionable as a result of the COM program, were:

1. The vendor's price lists in purchasing and purchase price controls appeared inadequate. This area should be reviewed for accuracy and improvement.
2. Concerning purchase order processing, review the open- and closed-order function for paperwork-processing improvements, and check other special orders in files.
3. Price check in payables: review the clerical function.
4. Security check on all product movement channels: part-number control is suspect.

5. Systems audit function of invoice billing is suspect.
6. Freight-processing procedures for all products need attention. This was an 80-percent distribution company, 20 percent manufacturing. Freight costs are of primary importance.
7. Returns of reject products should be analyzed.
8. Inventory control numbers (part numbers) must be assigned to every purchase and every sales product.
9. The systems billing error on special invoices could be a major dollar problem. This company should open the complete corporation special billing system for systems improvement analysis.

Looking at the Total COM Program

When I explained the principle of cash operations management in Chapter 3, several questions were raised. Now that we've seen how the testers problem developed in an actual COM business situation, let's see if the answers to these questions provide you with a better understanding of the values of COM in the business organization.

How Do We Find Additional Cash Profits?

The answer in Chapter 3 was that we find cash profits by conducting a COM program—*below the cash management level-line*. This is exactly what we did in the testers program.

Let's take it from step 1. When I searched for information about the $12,600 invoice, I did not find the answer in the accounting records. The answer came from an assistant production manager in the production plant. "Go to marketing," the man told me over the roar of the machines. Thus the answer was provided by an operations area: where physical dollars flow through the company.

Why Are These CMLL Dollars Important?

They are important for two reasons.

First, this is an expansive, dominant area for business profits. We analyzed the testers advertising program, which represented only a fraction of the total sales volume of the company. But look how large the tester dollars loomed. Originally there was a $115,000 investment. This grew to a $285,000 sales transaction in a $70-million corporation (less than one-half a percentage point of the total sales volume).

Second, once the profit problems were exposed, $84,037 showed up as a business loss. Because corporate profits were $2.5 million, the percentage of profit losses *expanded* to 3 percent of corporate profits. Now COM dollars exploded from 0.5 percent of corporate sales to 3 percent of total profits.

WHY? Because of *100-percent profit dollars*. When sales taxes were charged on the testers, and paid, that $7,200 came directly from company profits. When sales dollars were not invoiced for cash, accounts receivable had no chance to bring these dollars in for profits. The total amount to be billed on the invoice was lost—100-percent profit dollars—below the cash management level-line.

Where Do We Look for CMLL Dollars?

In the testers program, I looked at an unpaid invoice. I checked a couple of files, then conducted personal interviews. In time, by using COM to analyze the departments, I began to turn up profit losses.

Here were the important keys that opened profit ideas: (1) The interviews were most productive. They led me to John Teagarten, the sales service manager, who had answers to my questions. (2) The purchasing and cost accounting departments were key places because of the absence of an inventory control part number. (3) While accounting for units lost because of the part number, we discovered that EDP often had not billed for units. (4) Inventory control became a problem when the plants could not account for 8 percent of the units purchased. (5) Usage, freight, and returns became problems once the search was on for the lost units.

All of the above information was derived from company operations areas. The losses developed from physical dollars: (1) physical losses of products because of no inventory control number (operations); (2) sales wrote up a jinxed purchase order, and price references were lost (operations); (3) payables lacked sales tax payment knowledge and training (operations); (4) reject units were lost because of a communications pick-up problem from the plants (operations)—all the result of operations problems affecting physical dollars—below the CMLL.

How Much Profit Can Be Realized from CMLL Dollars?

For the most illustrative answer to this question, we must go back to the hourly rate of cash recovery. You will recall that the returns contributed $600 an hour in increased cash profits. If you keep an employee busy in this program for a period of one year, at $600 an hour, this profit-person will bring you more than a million dollars annually, assuming that your company is big enough to warrant this volume ($40 million sales volume annually will do it, and perhaps less). But even a cash return of $100,000 is a big lift for some companies, along with a bonus of $300,000 from improvements in systems and procedures. This is not uncommon in the COM program.

Another point: If your company is realizing a return of $600 an hour, it would make more business sense to assign an audit team to clear this cash in 3 months, not 12, for the cost-of-money factor. The interest on 1 million dollars for nine months can amount to $90,000 to $100,000 or more.

Again I emphasize that the biggest profit contribution is generally contributed through systems and procedures improvements in CMLL dollars. Cash-recovery returns are usually a one-time-through program, although improved systems and procedures, properly executed, should stop such annual cash losses.

Summary

Our approach to cash operations management has been, first, to explain that cash dollar profits do become lost in the business organization. The testers example illustrates that cash profits can fall through established systems and procedures. To identify exactly where these dollars fall, I have originated a division line in the organization identified as the cash management level-line. Profit items that fall below this line (CMLL) are the main topic of interest in this book.

In Figure 4.1 we follow up on the testers program. Note how the entire organization is represented through cash operations management.

In consulting work the COM profit loss is not an unusual occurrence. Companies lose cash through carelessness every day they are in business. The situation described above, as well as similar cash problems, has occurred in practically every business organization I have studied. I suspect that it is also happening in your company. The skills and ideas you pick up from this book will assist you in determining whether it is occurring in your own organization.

Let us end this chapter with the same statement we opened the chapter with, albeit abbreviated somewhat: "Early one morning, while shuffling through the large accounting department of the Cosmic Corporation, I stepped on a sheet of paper lying next to a payables desk. Reaching down to pick it up, I noticed that it was a Xerox copy of a six-month-old invoice." Through COM skills I turned this invoice into a windfall profit of $80,147 for the Cosmic Corporation. Turned over twice, this was more than $160,000 in additional profits, plus savings in systems and procedures.

One other note: Remember when I stopped to talk to the production manager in the plant? He gave me an important tip to another large COM cash-profit error. It was the asphalt consistency testers.

Hundreds and hundreds of asphalt testers were produced at this plant. Of course, the cost accountants had no part number assigned to this product either. It was an advertising project. The COM system continued indefinitely, as it will for all companies.

Figure 4.1   The entire organization COM testers problem

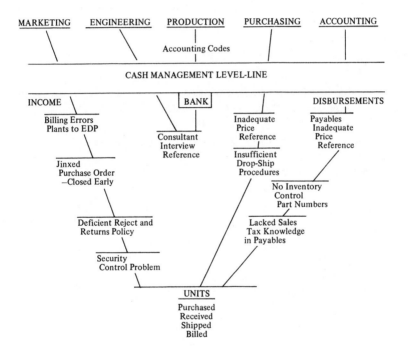

Questions on Chapter 4

GENERAL

1. What assurances are your employees giving the company president that they are accounting for and spending dollars accurately and properly?
2. Do you notice any "lack of financial interest" on the part of your employees in closing lost-dollars gaps?
3. Does your company have any departmental conflicts caused by special, unusual business transactions?
4. Do you have doubts about any of the controls on your EDP systems? Have you run a profit-audit analysis on these programs yet?
5. Are you giving your clerical employees "think time" on their jobs?

MARKETING

6. Do you make periodic audits of your billing system to ensure that all shipments are billed?
7. Do you have a special invoicing system? If so, has this system been audited to determine that all shipments are billed?
8. Who is responsible for merchandise handled in your company's advertising and sales promotion programs? Are there any special arrangements, such as in the testers program?
9. Who is responsible for purchasing advertising and sales promotion merchandise? Do they utilize the purchasing department for these purchases?

PURCHASING

10. Are you aware of the importance of clarity and terms when processing information from your company's purchase order forms?
11. Does your company have any "special purchase agreements" that vary from the path of normal purchasing or payables processing?
12. Do you understand how drop shipments can cause additional operations problems?
13. How can drop-shipment purchases cause duplicate billing?
14. What controls should be established in the receiving department on drop-shipment purchases? In purchasing? In payables?

ACCOUNTING

15. Do you see the difference between *physical* dollars flowing through an organization and *accounting coded* dollars?
16. Does your company general ledger have special miscellaneous

income–expense accounts established? What do the dollar amounts represent?

17. Do your cost accounting people make a point of applying an inventory control number to all purchased and manufactured products processed through your company?

18. Has your entire company EDP system had a thorough systems audit by an EDP audit-analysis expert?

PAYABLES

19. Does your payables department have numerous old, unpaid vendor invoices in the "work to be done file"? Are your vendors complaining about open invoices on their monthly statements?

20. Do your company supervisors use the criterion of "paperwork back-up" as a negative element of nonproduction? If so, have you audited your clerical functions for possible problem-prone transactions?

21. Is personnel turnover in payables causing a backup of paperwork? Is it causing account complaints from vendors?

22. Do you have any cases of specific vendors overcharging consistently for their products?

INVENTORY CONTROL

23. Do you have any products in your company now with *no* inventory control numbers?

24. Are you aware of the value of a manual inventory control function used *in addition to* a mechanized function? Used *instead of* a mechanized function?

25. Do you have your inventory on a perpetual inventory card-index system? Is it under stockroom control?

26. Are your fast-moving products turning over more than four times annually? If they turn over more than four times, do you have good economic controls on them to defray additional processing and carrying costs?

FREIGHT

27. Has your system for incoming and outgoing freight been analyzed for cost efficiency in the past 12 months?

28. Are too many freight collect bills causing extraordinary processing costs for your company?

29. Are your freight costs written into the prices and profits of your product? If not, will the freight cost make a drastic change in the profit markup on any particular product?

30. Is there reason to believe you may have duplicated shipping costs in your company?

RETURNS AND ALLOWANCES

31. How efficient are the return-goods systems and procedures in your company?
32. Does everyone involved in your sales program—employees as well as customers—know where and how to send a rejected or damaged product back to your company?
33. Has the expense of lost units and additional handling of reject units been written into the *profit structure* of your sales products? Are some products returned more often than others?

SECURITY

34. Do you have resalable products, in boxes, ready to go, stored near plant exits—all without reasonable security control?

5. Brain of a Computer: Financial Control of Cash-Payment Policies

Just after lunch one afternoon I walked into the accounts payable office of a Fortune 500 corporation in Chicago. I was there to conduct a study of the corporation's cash-payment policies.

The corporation became a conglomerate in 1968—the year of the conglomerates. Throughout the country there was a surge of corporations purchasing other companies. Three large divisions in this particular corporation had turned into twelve by this time, and the number of employees had increased to more than 2,300.

When I entered the slightly old-fashioned room decorated in the style of the early 1920s, I had an interesting surprise: there was only one desk in the room. Sitting behind it was a young woman. I introduced myself and asked if this was the accounts payable department.

"This is it, Mr. Sinn," she replied. Amazement showed in her face. She seemed dazzled that a complete stranger would intrude on her business domain. My first impression was that it was highly unusual for someone to stop by her desk.

"Where are all the people?" I asked, looking from side to side to give my question more meaning. Most accounts payables offices in large corporations have large staffs. As it turned out, this company was no different. In this corporation the accounts payable clerks were located in offices throughout the country. At the office I was in, a large volume of purchases of materials, as well as local purchases for this corporate office, were made through a centralized system.

"I'm the only person in accounts payable," the woman said, smiling. "What do you need?"

"I need to talk to you, that's what I need," I replied in jest. The comment seemed appropriate, for she was smiling. The ice of the consultant's approach was broken.

Patricia was her name. She pulled up a chair for me, and we began talking about her job. It wasn't easy for her; she wasn't accustomed to cross-examination. But I did what I could to make her feel at ease.

Finally a breakthrough. "Mr. Sinn, I've never had anybody talk to me about my job the way you talk to me," she explained. "No one ever told me I had to do anything other than match the invoice with the receiving ticket and write out the green ticket." The green ticket was the computer-payment form used by all the company's offices. The company had nineteen plants scattered across the country.

Things began to fall in place as I talked with Patricia about her work. Suddenly I noticed something peculiar. Here was someone with no training and no prior business experience. She was young—just a few months out of high school. I'd learned from the accounting records on the fourth floor that more than $6 million in purchases crossed her desk each year. Yet Patricia's desk was completely clear of paperwork. So were her file drawers. No receiving tickets were in her receiving file, and all her filed invoices were up to the current date. With the exception of some processed invoices in her outgoing box, ready to go to the computer for payment, there were no papers on or around this corporate office accounts-payable desk.

"Patricia, where is all your work right now—at this moment?"

"I'm done with my work. Everything is processed for today." It was 1:30 in the afternoon.

I reached for the invoices in the out box. The information I was looking for had to be there in that box. When searching for profit dollars, a consultant depends a great deal on instinct or so-called gut feeling. That gut feeling was coming on now; it didn't take long.

The Key to COM in Disbursements Control

On top of the stack of bills in the out box was a fire insurance invoice covering policies on some of the company's manufacturing plants. The premiums totaled $165,000, a huge figure by any standard, no matter what size company. I continued to study the invoice. An approval for payment had been signed by the assistant controller; the terms were one-third ($55,000) due May 31, one-third August 31, and one-third November 30. It was a lenient request—good terms.

Next I rolled back the green computer-payment form. That was the basis for keypunching the accounting records and payables checks. It had blanks for filling in accounting codes, amounts, vendor number, payment due date, and so forth. In my analysis I saw that the amount on the green ticket was $165,000; the date entered in the space labeled "Payment Due Date" was May 10—5 days away. Something was wrong here. In the complex world of big business and industry, an expensive error had just come to light.

"Patricia," I asked, "why are you paying the full $165,000 on this invoice when it's not due for seven months?"

She didn't flinch at the question. As a matter of fact, she gave me a quick, direct answer.

"All I have to do is put the pay date on the green slips, Mr. Sinn," she explained. "The computer pays the bills when they are due."

I looked at her in amazement. It was hard to believe what she had just said. "The computer pays them automatically according to due dates!" I blurted out.

"Yes sir. That's what they told me. You see, on this invoice"—she took the insurance invoice from my hand—"I put the next pay date in the payment due date space. The reason you put the pay date in is, the computer must have all the invoices by the next pay date. It then pays the invoices when they're due."

As best I could make out, Patricia thought the computer had the brain of a human. She thought it could read the face of the invoice, analyze the terms, and pay only the amount of money due at the time it was supposed to be paid.

Patricia wasn't alone in thinking this, however. The employees of the company, as well as employees of other companies throughout the nation, in both services and industry, have displayed the same confidence in the mechanical monster—the money-eating computer.

"Is this the way you process all your invoices, Patricia?" I asked. "Do you set them up so that all of your invoices are due by the next computer pay date?"

"Yes, I do, Mr. Sinn," she admitted confidently. This answered the question of why her desk and files were so clean; but that was only the beginning.

Patricia was right on one point. The computer *can* read, although it can do so only to the extent that it is programmed for such a task. On this particular program it could actually read "due dates," then automatically print a check to pay the appropriate invoices when they fell due. Patricia, however, was sending *pay* dates instead of *due* dates to the computer via the green ticket. This procedure would pay the invoice on the very next pay date—in the above instance, May 10.

This is where the *cash operations management* problem takes root. Patricia should have put the actual due date on the green slip (30 days for $55,000, due May 31). The next computer payment—June 10—would have paid the invoice automatically and properly. The remaining two payments, August 31 and November 30, should have separate green tickets made up, with their respective due dates listed. The computer would then hold the payments until September 10 and December 10.

Other invoices in Patricia's out box supported her comments. I had uncovered a major cash operations management profit-control problem; now I had to find the extent of the problem.

The Systems Loss in Cash-Payment Policies

The principle of cash operations management is to make good use of every possible dollar flowing through a business organization. The computer-payment example described above varied from this principle.

The problem basically was that invoices were being paid ahead of their due dates. This does not seem to be much of a problem on the surface, but when it affects the organization's system and procedures, profit dollars become an important issue.

Let's look at this from a COM program viewpoint. Initially, the *cash recovery* potential is not present. The cash profit potential is there, however, in the form of systems and procedure-improvement opportunities.

The best illustration of this is the $165,000 invoice. This insurance premium was to be paid in five days after receipt of the invoice. Additional consultant investigation confirmed this. But the terms on the invoice allowed up to seven months to pay the full amount.

Under Patricia's system, the $165,000 cash was to be pulled out of my client's bank seven months ahead of the time it was due to be paid. At the time the insurance agency cashes the check, my client will begin to accumulate cash losses in interest on the cost of money. This was at the rate of 12 percent annually on the $165,000. It was in the system. The losses could not be stopped until the system was corrected—until Patricia was instructed to use the *due date* on the computer green ticket instead of the next pay date.

Now, what were the cash losses on the $165,000? Interest at 12 percent on $165,000 paid on the agreed terms of the insurance invoice is worth $7,150 in the ever-important cost-of-money factor to my client. This was the amount of cash profit loss for the seven-month period. The $7,150 had slipped through the systems and fallen below the cash management level-line.

This is an important point. We have identified the loss in Patricia's area, but what have we learned? Certainly a $7,150, one-time loss would not warrant a monumental systems change in the organization's payment policies.

True, one-time losses should not require large systems changes. But the loss in the case described above is significant enough to cause us concern, not just for Patricia's department alone—though we should not overlook profit possibilities there. But this corporation had 19 plants spread around the country, and they were all using the same payment system. This is the vast profit potential area that became my concern. Suppose one-time losses were occurring in all the plants, all year long, and were compounding profit loss upon profit loss in this company? This was where the one-time cash loss could become a cash operations management systems nightmare. Under these circumstances, a monumental systems change was warranted.

Analysis Review

For the purposes of reader reference, let us pause here to analyze what has been done up to this point and to study how the review was conducted.

Step 1: The consultant's assignment was to review the cash-payment policies of the corporation.

Step 2: I reviewed the complete accounts-payable system in the corporate accounting office. This included introduction to the payables vendor balances, invoice batch processing, total dollar volume processed, and computer involvement.

Step 3: I interviewed the person in charge of corporate payables and investigated files, invoices, and so on. I looked for exceptions to normal procedures in cash-payment policies.

Step 4: I came to conclusions about the findings in the review. The initial review isolated three problem areas: (1) procedures: payables invoices were being paid before their due dates; (2) a computer program loophole: this allowed open access to cash disbursements, which meant that any person who submitted an invoice to the computer, with a green ticket attached, could receive a negotiable check, in effect, freedom to write a check at will; (3) employee training: Patricia, a new employee, had not been given the required training support.

The Cash Operations Management Approach

I went into action. Consultants become consultants because they take that extra step. The fact that a huge computer-control gap existed in the corporation's main office was merely the first step.

Each of the corporation's 19 plants had an accounts-payable office. The company offices were highly diversified except for their central payables-payment system on the computer. The primary question, then, was what the other plants were doing. Were they, too, taking the easy way out and paying invoices ahead of their due dates? There were no written procedures to prevent the extension of the problem; so it was indeed possible.

After discussing this new-found point with management, I began an extensive investigation of the corporation's complete cash-payment system. My approach was to home in on the two large cash payments sent from the computers at the home office on the 10th and 25th of each month.

We immediately put a hold on the May 10 payment; management was not to release any checks until cleared to do so by my review. At the same time, I requested a computer printout of vendor invoices scheduled to be paid on the 10th and 25th.

Next came the tedious and cumbersome task of determining the actual due dates on each invoice scheduled to be paid. This required finding the terms of payment for each individual vendor, listing the amounts due, and recording the information in chronological order by due date. It was a manual task. Because of a lack of on-line information, the computer could not help.

The surprising results of the analysis dazzled the corporation's executives. Approximately $1.2 million had been paid up to 20 to 30 days ahead of terms! More than $250,000 was scheduled for payment 90 days ahead of the time it should have been paid. In terms of cash-profit loss in the cost of money, my client was losing approximately $112,000 interest in annual corporate profits.

A cash-profit loss of $112,000 was discovered by processing an accounts-payable invoice. The method of detection would seem to be simple, and it was—to a degree. It was simple except for the common sense and imagination required in follow-through on good business decisions. These are two commodities that seem hard to come by in some parts of big business today.

In retrospect, an error of $112,000 in either business or industry is not a simple matter. At that rate of loss, such an error becomes complex and serious. It becomes more so when two or more of these $112,000 errors fall out of a company's system.

More often than not, multiple errors will happen in companies. The important thing to know ahead of time is the extent of the problems. Be certain there is no "chain reaction of errors" in your systems. This is what we looked for in the company under discussion.

As we will see in this book, case histories illustrate how the simpliest of business functions—a payables invoice, a stack of sales invoices, even a box of trash on a factory floor—can lead to amazing new profits because of a chain reaction of cash losses.

COM Dollars and Ideas from the Analysis

Now let us return to the corporate accounts-payable office in Chicago. The profit loss of $112,000 was only part of the values contributed by the cash operations management system. Let us examine the problems one by one, as illustrated below.

A $2-Million Checkbook

Top management people had not concentrated on cash controls of accounts-payable. The computer green ticket was a "crooked man's answer to a vacation in paradise."

When the green ticket was filled in at the proper spaces and fed into the computer, it automatically released a printed check. This check was signed and ready to process at a bank. It was even put in an envelope without further audit.

Further increasing the profit risk, this corporate bank account consistently *carried a $2 million balance* throughout the year. This corporation gave the responsibility for a $2-million checkbook to an 18-year-old fresh out of high school with no prior business experience. At times, it seems almost amazing that some businesses can stay afloat.

Accounting Versus Purchasing—The Perennial Conflict

Accounts payable was under the jurisdiction of the purchasing department at this corporate location. The purchasing department did not want the accounts-payable function in its office, and for good reason: it meant more work. The accounting department did not want it for the same reason. Both departments were ignoring the control factor. Neither wished to ignore that factor, but neither did purchasing or accounting want to do anything about it. Thus, in their failure to accept responsibility, both departments relegated cash profits to a back seat, behind office politics or just plain laziness.

Tossing the payables responsibility about was only the surface wound. A larger, profit-tainted problem now became evident, as I have noted in other organizations: *Distinctly bad relations between large-company accounting and purchasing departments is an ever-present battle.* This unfortunate situation, though often unrecognized, does occur between the accounting and purchasing departments of large corporations. The people in these departments often antagonize each other until a communications breakdown becomes a profit problem. It is not uncommon for the purchasing department to be located as far as possible from the accounting department—when, according to economic logic, they should be side by side.

Accounts-Payable Control

The combination of accounts payable, purchasing, shipping, and receiving—all at the disposal of the purchasing manager—at the very least, eliminates the checks and balances of good business-accounting procedures. Doesn't it follow that our Chicago corporation had just such a circumstance and situation: the "crooked man's answer to a vacation in paradise."

No one individual should be in a position to order materials for a company, attest to their having been received, approve payment for them, and authorize their shipment out of a company's custody after payment has been received. Because this client company allowed the circumstance to arise, it opened itself as an easy target for fraud.

Employee Training

Specific guidelines exist in companies for training new employees. Of course, policies vary from company to company. This subject is outside our area of discussion in this book; when employee training affects cash profit-loss, however, it becomes important to everyone.

In the case of the Chicago corporation, a particular employee was not the problem. The perennial conflict between purchasing and accounting led to a deficiency that was caused more immediately by lack of training of the employee. Neither the purchasing department nor the accounting department wanted to train Patricia or the payables clerks who had preceded her. Accounting did everything it could to convince purchasing that the payables clerk was purchasing's responsibility. Purchasing, on the other hand, considered the job an accounting one. As it turned out, Accounting agreed to give Patricia limited training, and purchasing was persuaded to allow her to work in their office. The result was that she was taught the three basic match-ups: the invoice, the receiving report, and the purchase order.

The *paperwork value* of materials and services that crossed Patricia's desk was not emphasized. As someone just out of high school, she could not be expected to realize the need to attain corporate profits.

The Issue of Minorities

Another issue was involved, one that made a difference in this case. It was an issue that was taken seriously. The company needed additional members of minorities. Patricia was black. No one in management, personnel—no one anywhere in the company—was about to terminate a black employee without just cause.

The first thing that occurred to the people in accounting and purchasing after my review was that they would have to fire Patricia. Supposedly, according to management, all aspects of accounts payable had been presented to her. The lack of interest on management's part, however, caused Patricia to lose a sense of urgency in her job. Gradually she began to overlook details. Still, management wanted to make every possible effort to keep her.

I made a suggestion, which the company accepted, that some consultant training in specifics be given Patricia. Accounting was to follow up with training at frequent intervals. Patricia's work soon began to take form and direction.

Systems Changes Through COM Recommendations

Let us sum up what has been discussed in this chapter by describing the results of developing cash operations management skills in the corporation under discussion. This can best be done by listing changes made by the client as a result of the management consultant's recommendations.

Pay-Date Forms Change

The corporate controller changed the payment date box to read "Due Date" on the green ticket form for the computer—an easy, simple forms adjustment. But keep in mind that a 2-inch firing pin can fire a shell from a 30-foot cannon. In this instance, it was an annual, profit-loss explosion of $112,000.

In all future payment transactions, payables employees were instructed to determine the invoice *due dates* as a manual function. The due dates were then recorded on the green tickets. Next the computer would take over and separate the invoices according to their proper pay dates. Using the computer as adjusting robot brain was discontinued. The computer provided the mechanical assistance—as it is designed to do—and the employees apply the brainpower.

Management Control of Payments

The $1.2 million was shifted ahead by 20 to 30 days and placed in a savings account. The invoices set up for payment during that period were held and paid 20 to 30 days later on their accurate due dates.

The new due-date system took over from that point, which held the $1.2 million in the bank account permanently. This established a control situation whereby an invoice would never be set up before the due date and payment would always follow the due date. Management now had control of payments. Until now, the numerous company accounts-payable clerks had controlled the dates of payment. The costly result of this practice was loss of interest on the cost of money. Cash profits had escaped the bank at the rate of $112,000 a year—below the *cash management level-line.*

Accounts Payable Back to Accounting

The accounting department reclaimed the accounts-payable function from the purchasing department. The long-standing conflict (many business people would say *"eternal* conflict") between the two departments had been costly.

The important improvement here was the security of implementing new, basic accounts-payable controls. The functions of buying, receiving, paying, and shipping were separated from the dominant purchasing department.

Note here that purchasing can have the accounts-payable function, but accounting must follow up conscientiously with internal audit. What does this cause? Right: more conflict between the two departments.

Summary

Today, when I call that Chicago corporation, Patricia answers the phone as the receptionist. Her heartfelt hello always exudes warmth. I get the impression that she may be saying thanks for the special attention paid her as a result of my visit to her accounts payable department years ago. Looking back, we know she could not be faulted because of her work. She had too much going for her. Now she is an excellent, long-term, respected employee.

A final note but an important one. A number of years have passed, and the $112,000 annual cash recovery has now grown to more than $700,000 in additional assets for the corporation.

Questions on Chapter 5

GENERAL

1. Who can your company president depend on to spend the company's money efficiently? How does the information given in this chapter apply to your company's cash operations payment and purchasing policies? Following are questions that will serve to qualify your organization's controls of cash disbursements. Use this list to determine if there are things you can do to improve your company's cash profits through cash operations management.

MANAGEMENT

2. Who makes the payment-date decision in your company, management or clerical employees?
3. Are your payments to vendors ahead of their due dates? Have you run a detailed invoice analysis on this subject during the past 12 months?
4. Are decisions to spend large sums of money handled by top executives? Do they sign approvals? Do these executives get the checks back for audit before the checks are sent to vendors?
5. Does your company have specific guidelines for training new employees with cash-operations-management responsibilities? Who is responsible for payables? Receivables? Purchasing?
6. Is your purchasing department located near your accounting department?
7. Are your employees in purchasing and accounting compatible, to the extent that their responsibilities do not conflict? Do you have specific written procedures covering this area?
8. How much money is spent annually in each departmental or functional area?

PAYABLES AND PURCHASING

9. What is the minimum amount on an invoice that can be paid without middle-management approval? Before or after payables processing?
10. Who is personally supervising the cash payment system in your company? Is it the person who releases the cash that pays the bills? Does he or she recognize the value of payment guidelines, of prices, contracts, discounts, freight, and so on?
11. Have you established a regulated, due-date-payment procedure in your payables system? A written procedure?
12. Do your accounts-payable clerks understand how policies and procedures for payables are processed through the computers? Are there any loopholes, such as depending on the computers to do the work, that have not been plugged?
13. Are payables systems forms adequate for the current on-line systems? Should they be revised? Can money-saving ideas be developed by using new payables forms (payables voucher form, debit memos, returned materials forms, and so on)?
14. What relationship exists between the supervisor and the payables clerks? Does the supervisor answer questions for and give advice to the clerks regularly? Do they have a good, verbal, communicative relationship that reflects a positive attitude in the employees?

15. Are good payment procedures followed by your payables department? Are all prices, quantities, receipts—the basics—checked?
16. Has your employees' accounts-payable training program been updated in the past 12 months? Are your employees qualified to process $30 million dollars' worth (your company volume) of your company's money annually?

SECURITY

17. What security precautions are written into the basic accounts-payable procedures? Can the person originating the purchase order also receive materials, approve payment, and authorize outgoing shipments?
18. What security precautions are taken on checks distributed from the computer? Are they checked before they are mailed?
19. What precautions are taken to prevent an employee from submitting a bogus invoice into the system and getting it paid?

6. Wheels Grinding Out Dollars: Purchasing, Inventory Control, and Cash

He measures by millionths of an inch
Knows ball bearings from spiral gearings,
Chain transmission, heat treatment of steel
Speeds and feeds of automatic screw machines
With pistol grip and trigger switch
Carl Sandburg

Chicago, with its industrial wealth of production capacity, as a toolmaker, is Sandburg's city of gears grinding steel against steel. "Stormy, husky, brawling, City of the big shoulders".

The tone and emotion of Sandburg's words are almost real as you walk the oil-laden paths winding through huge factories. The noise can be overbearing; the smell can go home with you at night. But to see the products come off the lines one by one is majestic. One is awed by the rhythm, the sights and sounds of a manufacturing plant.

A salesperson walking through a plant shows a customer the beauty of the manufactured product. When an accountant goes through, he or she is checking inventories. The consultant, however, is looking for dollars—dollars that escape the profit in manufacturing the product.

This consultant's trip seemed cold and calculating compared to Sandburg's. To recover another profit-making example from my file of case histories on cash operations management, however, I had to get at the facts, and the facts are that it was indeed a trip through an enormous production plant one day that drew my attention to something unusual.

The constant noise from the machines was deafening. I concentrated on some resin-bonded grinding wheels I had spotted in various places as I walked along the aisles of the factory. The wheels were stacked in large numbers under machines, while many others were stored in dark, dusty corners. I walked over to talk to one of the machine operators standing nearby. "Why are these grinding wheels under the machines?" I yelled over the din.

"That's where we keep the wheels for the machines," the operator answered.

My amazement was increasing fast. That was no place to store production grinding wheels. From the way the operator explained it, though, it sounded as if that was standard company procedure. "Do you think that's a good way to store the wheels?" I yelled.

"Hell, no. They get broken. They get lost. People steal them for the other machines. Who knows where they go. But that's not my problem."

"So, where do you get new wheels when you run out?"

"I go and tell Sam in Purchasing to order me another dozen. He can get 'em in two days."

The machine operator sounded convincing. He obviously knew the purchasing area well. But then, production people thrive on going up front to the offices. Any excuse to get up there is a good excuse. It's a kind of rest and recuperation for them; it gets them out of the production pits. I can't blame them; but it's costly, especially if the automatic machinery should go beserk while the operator is passing the time of day in the purchasing office.

"How long will a dozen grinding wheels last you?" I inquired, referring to what the operator had said about a two-day order.

"Couple weeks."

"Do you ever run out?" I asked.

"Yeah, once in a while—when he can't get 'em soon enough."

I nodded my head as though I understood, then walked back to a dark corner where some grinding wheels were stored.

While looking over the stacks of wheels, I recalled an incident that had happened years ago, when I was a boy. My father had a farm machinery business in Paulding, Ohio. A plowshare I was sharpening one day jammed the edge of a large, churning grinding wheel while it was spinning at high speed on the grinder. The wheel burst, and pieces flew everywhere in the back of the shop. It's a wonder I and other people there were not hurt, or even killed. When the dust had settled and he knew everyone was safe, my father explained how expensive grinding wheels were. That was in the late 1940s; they are much more expensive today.

My imagination began to compound dollars as I looked around the factory. Grinding wheels seemed to be everywhere. I came to the disheartening conclusion that machine operators were going directly to the purchasing agent to order a two-weeks supply for their machines. This company's sales volume was $16 million. Grinding wheels were their primary manufacturing expense item, yet it seemed that the company had no inventory control system. Without question, I could see a cash operations management problem emerging. This company needed some consultant analysis work. Apparently the problem had escaped the trends and guidelines detection of monthly financial statements. It appeared that physical dollars were falling below the cash management level-line.

The Initial Analysis

Initially, I needed pertinent information, as soon as possible, that would show the magnitude of the problem. The answer would be found under "grinding wheel purchases" in the manufacturing operating expense ledgers. In addition, inventory controls and usage calculations would have to be audited to determine if they were operating efficiently. Then, of course, storage controls and facilities had to be checked, which would complete the survey of obvious problems that had surfaced during my walk through the plant.

The more obscure problems involved determining whether accounts-payable controls were operating efficiently and whether good pricing practices were being followed. Written procedures for controlling all of these areas would also become a question.

The Analysis Interviews

Production

My search first took me to the office of the production manager. There I wanted to find out how many machines there were in my client's two plants. This was the easiest part of the assignment. It is the easy interviews that sometimes bring the most useful information, however, particularly in the production areas of an organization. Production people want things to work smoothly, and they do want to make improvements. Their suggestions, they feel, will be blocked by the political hierarchy of the organization. Thus a negative attitude often develops among them. Such negative attitudes have cost organizations a lot of dollars through lack of employee-management communication.

"The total number of production machines comes to over 120 units of various shapes and sizes," the production manager told me.

All of the machines were designed to make the same basic products. These 120 machines filled requirements and specifications for approximately 225 different combinations of types and sizes of grinding wheels used on the machines.

"Who has the responsibility for buying grinding wheels in the company?" I asked.

"Sam Dixon—over in Purchasing. All wheel-purchase request forms go to him. "I've been here only two months, so I'm not sure who submits the requests. But the supervisors are supposed to, I think."

Uncertainty showed in his voice. Those two months on the job could mean that the company had had problems with the previous production manager. The current production manager as much as said so, and it was later confirmed in a management meeting. The production manager did not know what kind of purchase control system they had on wheels. If I had questioned him any further, it would have pushed him. So I backed off. I would need him on my side later. His final comment was: "Just so Sam gets the wheels to us when we need them."

The possibility that there were overcharges on the cost of the wheels had not occurred to the production manager. These added costs alone could completely strip his production jobs of a profit markup. This is not to take anything away from the production manager; in time, I learned that he was doing excellent work in his position. He had ambition and the desire to do a good job. His predecessor had left him with a tremendous challenge, and cash operations management controls in purchasing were not high on his list of priorities.

This is a typical situation. Cash-management problems in operational areas seldom make the priority lists of employees. Such problems should be uppermost on their minds, however, because that's a profit area. In most cases even accounting employees fail to emphasize this area; all the other departments in the organization feel that Accounting is where cash management begins. They are not altogether wrong. But then, who is left to do the work? Whom can the company president depend on to tell him or her whether the company's money is being spent properly? The need becomes evident for a cash operations management profit program in business organizations, one that can be handled by a "profit person."

Accounting

Like the production manager of this company, the controller was also a very busy person. The controller was involved in the installation of a computerized billing program. Indeed, it was necessary; the company had lines and lines of products to type on customer invoices. The controller was also responsible for credit and collections, payroll, general and cost accounting, taxes, financial statements, and, naturally, accounts payable. These are typical responsibilities of a controller. Not included, of course, were the numerous hours each week spent in management meetings. Keeping this kind of a schedule, is it any wonder that the controller could not find the time to get into a COM program?

So, what did we have in this company's accounting department other than an outline of the controller's duties? One positive point—in the cash operations area—was consistency in billing controls and follow up. My client was on top of the billing function. The company had placed emphasis on not losing a dime during its conversion to computers, and it had been successful.

A point to be made here is that billing controls are a direct-line function. Accounting people generally do not mind working on accounts receivable, because the detail is rather clean, from cradle to grave. There aren't as many auditables as there are in purchasing and accounts payable. As an example, basically one price list is used to bill customers, whereas many price lists must be used for the numerous vendors in payables. This is not to say that things cannot go wrong in the billing area. When billing goes wrong, it does so on a large scale. The bottom falls out. But this usually happens in the mechanical end of billing, not so much in a consistent pricing structure. A later chapter gives more cash-management background in billing and accounts-receivable profits.

What, then, were the facts in Accounting on grinding wheels? The most pertinent fact was the volume of purchase dollars.

As a matter of judgment, with the expectation of high dollar volume, one would think that Accounting's general ledger would have a breakdown of purchases of grinding wheels. But don't count on it. General ledger information is just what it says: *general*. Wheels are a manufacturing expense item, not a raw material. Raw materials are more likely than manufacturing expense items to be recorded in detail. Here, there was no accumulated breakdown of annual purchases in the accounting records. What information there was, was mixed with other materials, in monthly accounting accruals; and cutoffs were not clear. This is true in most companies, especially the smaller, growing ones. Finding factual cumulative totals with desired cutoffs in general ledgers is practically impossible; that's why accountants are not likely to conduct a COM program. They will analyze everything in terms of general-ledger entries and accruals, whereas consultants rely specifically on *actual cash transactions* off disbursement and billing records.

Thus the only course open to this client was to find annual purchases of grinding wheels through actual payments to vendors—vendors' regularly issued checks.

COM Note

It is important to understand, as a matter of interest, that the *vendor's check*, with invoices attached, is a prominent tool in company cash operations management and cash recovery. It holds a world of financial and operational information about organizational profits. Understandably, it is recognized as the ultimate financial trail to cash actually spent. A simple observation, yes, but one never to be underestimated in the act of recovering cash profits.

In this company, the vendor's check was the only means of locating the annual $510,000 in grinding wheel purchases, as well as determining usage of the wheels. This revealed a half-million dollar base for analysis by the COM program. My next consulting step wasn't far off.

Purchasing

Purchasing was my next stop. It was the core of my review in the company. I had learned what was involved and was ready, in terms of justifying my presence, to inquire about the grinding wheels.

The Sam Dixon Interview

Sam Dixon's office was practically a hole in the wall. It was located in a production area of the factory, not surprisingly the farthest office from Accounting. The office was in a dismal area. It had a darkened entrance from the production plant, the lighting was bad, and overall it seemed a bad working atmosphere. Inside the office, however, the atmosphere was somewhat better. Despite being so close to the production machines, it was clean and well dusted. There was no debris or old parts lying around, and the office even had a small picture window overlooking a well-manicured lawn in front of the building.

Sam Dixon's office reflected the habits and attitudes of its occupant. Dixon was a neat man in his late forties with a dated appearance and a short haircut. He was meticulous in keeping himself and his environment. Dixon took care of the little things. The two primary concerns of his were to keep track of lead pencils in the offices and to appear busy.

"Can I help you with anything?" Sam Dixon asked as I entered his office.

"I'm looking for Sam Dixon," I announced. I was in a vested suit and tie, apparently overdressed for this office.

"You got 'im." Dixon was sitting behind an old steel-gray desk. A surprised look was on his face. His voice had a phony but at the same time authoritative tone. In time, as a layman in the field, I identified these two parts of his personality. The authoritativeness derived from the responsibility of the $8 million in purchases that were channeled through his office; the phoniness came from his years of stagnant business existence. Dixon had been taken off the production lines 15 years ago and promoted to head of Purchasing. Sales were low at the time—less than $1 million dollars. Now the sales volume of the company was $16 million. The company still had the same purchasing and inventory control systems, now more than 15 years old and obviously outdated—and they still had Sam Dixon. Over the 15-year period he had progressed no further than had his company's systems.

After introducing myself I asked about the purchases of grinding wheels. My strategy was to get Dixon's thoughts on the control of wheel purchases and on inventory usage. My main purpose was to see if he thought his present purchasing system was sufficient. He did not waste any time in telling me.

"Sure we have a good system," he said. "I can get wheels delivered in two days." Obviously he had either misunderstood the question or did not recognize what a purchasing system was.

"What kind of quantities are you talking about?" I asked.

"Any quantities!" Sam blurted out with a smirk on his face. I sensed a tone of animosity in his answers. "We have some on blanket orders."

The term *blanket orders* referred to purchase orders for large quantities of one or more items supplied to industry and service companies. It's an ideal purchasing method as long as you acquire the lowest possible purchase price and control the negotiated points on the purchase order, such as price, quantity, delivery, and freight costs.

"How many different wheels do you have on blanket orders? A general figure—fifty, eighty percent?"

Dixon did not like the question. One of the machine operators had just come into the office. I got the impression that Dixon thought my question had hurt his image. My presence had made him look bad in front of the operator. Dixon had established a dynasty there in the purchasing office. Unfortunately for the company and its owners, the president and members of the board, Dixon's dynasty was arranged around one of the largest profit areas of the company.

"I can't answer a question like that," Sam said. "I just know we get good prices on the blanket orders."

Though quite unqualified, this was his first comment on prices. Nevertheless, I jumped on the price comment. This was what I needed. "How good are the prices? Can you show me your price list for wheels?" I asked—rather candidly, I thought.

"Are you kid'n?" Dixon blurted out. "We have over a hundred different wheels. How am I going to keep price lists on them?"

Sam had just told me what I wanted to know: no price lists on wheel purchases. "How do you know you're paying the right price on the wheels?" I said abruptly. "Aren't you responsible for auditing the prices on vendor invoices?"

The questions went directly to the jugular. His face went blank. Meekly he followed with another comment: "I keep the prices on those cards over there." He pointed to a box on a table across the room. "That's how I know I'm paying the right prices."

"Are they kept up to date, then?" I asked. Apparently Dixon had answered the last question he intended to answer. Aware of the extent of the interrogation I had just subjected him to—probably something no one had done to him before on this job—I figured it was time to back off.

Apparently so did Dixon. His emotions had peaked, which showed in his flushed face. "Wait just a minute," he said. "This machine operator needs wheels. He's making money for the company." Abruptly he turned his chair, avoiding my stare, and engaged in petty conversation with the operator.

My presence in the purchasing office was not to investigate the mating calls of northern Illinois frogs. I was there to make money, too. A program designed to bring about a financial turnaround in profit was already a possibility here, and I could have laid it out for Sam Dixon. He was testing the Consultant's Code of Conduct for treatment of client employees. The man was so high on his purchasing pedestal that he didn't understand—or care—that I was the president's man.

By this time in the interview, I had concluded that this man was an incompetent. Years before, he had been promoted beyond his level of competence in the company. It was now clear to me that Dixon would lose his title as the company's primary purchaser. But I still hoped to be able to suggest that he be kept on in a lower capacity, so that his experience and knowledge of the company's production materials could be put to good use.

In the meantime, it was necessary to keep communications open with Sam; I would need him for identifying other problem areas. I ignored his sarcasm and continued my inquiry with another comment. "Sam," I interrupted, "direct me to your purchase orders on grinding wheels, and I'll be content." He did. He had a woman in the office show me the purchase order file. She also gave me the index card file. Even though it was incomplete as a detailed, informal record of wheel purchases, this file was the key—my first step toward discovering a cash operations profit contribution.

Grinding Wheels COM System

Once the COM research program was underway, I found that my original conclusions were realistic. This company had myriad cash problems. They were so numerous that, to define them, we had to separate them into categories.

The biggest problems were basically as expected: inventory control and purchase procedures. This, of course, led to poor pricing and in general extended into poor systems and procedure controls in cash operations management. Storage and physical product control added to my client's woes.

In the basic COM program we had success with numerous cash recoveries, for several reasons. Similarly, with systems and procedures problems, recoveries were widespread. But let's not waste any more words on explanation; let's identify the major areas at fault in cash losses, then see where the losses fell out of the system—below the cash management level-line.

Critical Profit Areas Ignored

Initially we recognized a number of critical areas in cash operations management that required immediate attention. These areas fell into four basic categories:

1. *No inventory control.* There were 225 different wheel applications. Thousands of wheels were purchased—more than $500,000 in annual volume—yet there were no records of inventory or usage to guide purchase transactions.
2. *No purchase price controls.* A large number of wheels was purchased annually, yet a major portion were bought on a single-item basis. Contract prices and volume discounts should have been applicable.
3. *Poor purchase procedures.* There was no purchase plan. Although this was a large company, machine operators left their jobs to go to the purchasing department to place wheel orders for the next two weeks. Where were the purchase and production records for controlling these second-rate procedures?
4. *No stockroom control.* Wheels were lying all over the production plant floors. How could a company account for 225 different wheel models if there was no central location, indicated on an organized recorded plan, for dispensing the wheels? The fact is, they could not account for the physical disposition of the wheels. Physical control had to be implemented to stop dollar losses of inventory control, breakage, and theft.

When all four of the above are found in one corporate procurement system, there can be no question that cash problems will occur. These are primary purchase functions in an organization, and none of them may be ignored. Now that we know they *were* ignored in my client's company, let's look at some examples of the cash and systems profit losses so that you may relate them to your own organization's systems.

No Inventory Control on Wheels

There simply was no inventory control on grinding wheels in this company. This is somewhat difficult to comprehend, particularly since a $510,000 purchase volume was involved.

Perhaps Sam Dixon had some kind of system—a "feel"—for purchasing these wheels. Such a system may have worked earlier, when the business was small, but now, at a sales level of $16 million, the company needed sophisticated systems.

Statistics on the COM Review

Let's look at the statistics on the inventory of grinding wheels after my review. This should give a total picture of why a company needs inventory control.

1. Out of a total $125,000 grinding-wheel inventory, 49%—more than $60,000 of the stock—represented a 1-year supply or more. Management requested a 90-day supply (three to four turnovers) after the controls I suggested were implemented. Thus the inventory was overstocked by approximately $45,000.
2. Of 225 wheel sizes in stock there was better than a year's supply (39%) of 82 sizes. An additional note: 42 of the 82 sizes carried balances of more than $500 in value, and some as high as $2,500.
3. In line with these statistics, the current stock items represented $65,000 in inventory. This meant that the $65,000 was turning over an average of seven times per year to make the $510,000 of annual purchase volume. Through our statistics, however, we knew that there were many more turnovers than were reflected in the average. Orders were put through in ridiculously low quantities and at excessively high process costs.

Multiple Effect of Processing Costs

An example may serve to illustrate this inventory control meaning more vividly. Let's follow up on the recent purchase history of grinding-wheel size 12X.150X3. This is a good example of how not to control the purchase of a multiline product. In addition, we will see how COM profit losses occurred through inadequate inventory controls.

Grinding wheel 12X.150X3 is a resin-bonded wheel. It has a specification application of 33A1006 R4-22X173. If this description and part number seem overlabeled, they are meant to be. This item represents only a tiny part of a COM program, and I do not want to leave the impression that this program has simple solutions. This is only one of 225 wheels that required detailed analytical work.

After determining a price base for the wheel, I headed for the accounts-payable department. The price base (the company used individual wheel contracts) went back 15 months, so I reviewed 15 months of paid invoices. The research was lengthy. Only one grinding wheel was charged on each invoice, and 225 wheels were included, with as many as seven turnovers a year.

In my research, through stacks and stacks of invoices, I found purchases of the wheel had been made 12 times over a 15-month period, or 9.6 turnovers per year. The most that were needed was five orders (an order every 3 months), which would yield a 90-day stock.

If you needed to process only 5 purchase orders through your system, why process 12? That increased the process work by 240 percent. The answer turned out to be that the company's employees did not know how many wheels they needed at the time of purchase.

This raised another question: Why didn't the employees know how many wheels they needed? The answer—*management and the employees simply did not provide guidelines of inventory control for their company.*

The High Cost of Poor Inventory Control

What did this lack of inventory control cost the company, in terms of cash operations profit dollars? The answer is, plenty. There is tremendous value in a good business inventory control system.

What were some of the lost values in this grinding wheel program? There were many. Following are some of them:

1. The lack of inventory control caused additional processing costs. If you process 12 purchase orders when 5 will do the job, you are increasing your workload by 240 percent. The additional process expenditures alone—in purchasing, receiving, payables, and freight— cost this company more than $35,000 each year. This was at $16-million sales volume. If the sales volume increases, processing costs will increase at a similar rate.
2. Because of inadequate inventory control, the company was charged high prices on large-quantity orders, and it paid them. They were charged a certain price for 100 wheels when they could have ordered 300, 500, or even 1,000 and paid a different, lower price. The breakdown of inventory control contributed to this problem.
3. Rush orders were caused by not knowing wheel usage and the current inventory balances. These "rushes" meant premium prices in addition to disruption of the flow of materials in the production department.

Every business organization concerned about profits in the area of inventory control must have a product-by-product grasp of what materials are flowing through its plant or plants. In the following pages is offered a system and a guide designed to increase organizational profits through cash operations management in inventory control. It is in the form of a product purchase-control manual supported by the theory of the "part number principle" (PNP), a term that is discussed in detail in Chapter 7.

Product Purchase Control Manual

The purchase control manual is a usage-control manual intended to develop the product-by-product function in a business organization. Its main purpose is to provide at a glance a usage and price record for the managers in an organization: production, inventory control, materials control, payables, and purchasing, as well as other production people such as the stockroom clerk and the assistant production manager.

It is important for these people to know the price and the inventory and usage status of the products or raw materials moving through the production plant. The amount of money involved will put emphasis on their work in this area. The manual provides employees with this information.

Another good reason for using this manual is the labor-saving possibilities it suggests. Better use of a production manager's time is a good example. When requisitions cross his or her desk, the manual will provide an immediate, fingertip reference for usage, price, specification, and current inventory. Until now, such a responsibility was ignored in this company until the production manager got around to it, and sometimes that time never came. Thus, if a problem existed, the potential profit loss was not revealed.

In addition, this manual provides a base for reporting to the company vice-president or president, people who are also concerned with inventory levels. Within moments the manual can help them produce an inventory overstock report.

Uses The product purchase control manual is designed for various uses. It has all the answers for product-by-product control—which is the ultimate answer for maximum profits in materials control. In another chapter I refer to the part number principle, or PNP, which will identify the theory behind product-by-product control. Some important uses of the manual follow. The manual:

1. Identifies suppliers and specifications quickly, by part number and specification.
2. Identifies slow usage before inventory build-up.
3. Gives price comparisons at a glance.
4. Gives the supply on hand, in months, and updates the figure quarterly.
5. Indicates that supplies are low (if the tickler file misses this) and reminds the manager to reorder.
6. Provides a basis for reporting inventory stock immediately.

The product control manual contains the simplest business form imaginable. Each product in the manual is controlled by a single loose-leaf page placed in numerical order in a three-ring binder. It is adapted to replacing or correcting a part-number history when necessary. The basic format is similar to the grinding-wheel form shown in Figure 6.1.

Figure 6.1   Basic product control form

PURCHASE CONTROL MANUAL

Explanation: The purchase control manual is a usage control manual. Its primary purpose is to provide an at-a-glance usage and price record for the managers of the organization. It is intented primarily to provide an answer to maximum profits in materials control.

FORM: _____

PRODUCT NO. _____ Date _____

DESCRIPTION _____

Vendors, Specifications, Prices, Effective dates

INVENTORY STATUS

Date	Supply on Hand	Inventory	Usage:	
			Mo.	Yr.

At the top of the form is a line for entering the description of the product. This applies to any type of multiple-line product: glass-cuts, extrusions, purchased parts, and so on. The form is designed to incorporate every application or situation involving a product. The date at the right is for entering the date on which the form originated.

The area below the top line is the vendor's. The name of each supplier of a product is listed in a separate column, along with the product's specifications. The prices of products, copied from vendors' price lists, are listed by their effective dates, below the specifications area. I cannot emphasize too strongly the importance of recording these prices from actual, *negotiated* vendors' price lists and *not* from prices charged. Among other things, this manual is designed to be an accurate price reference for purposes of audit or for normal use in payables, purchasing, or production functions. Prices must be updated immediately after being announced by the supplier.

The area at the bottom of the form is reserved for inventory status. This is the key area for developing facts about the PNP. Here are shown the in-depth movement of a purchased or manufactured part in your raw material inventory. Simply by investigating the monthly or quarterly inventory balance, you can determine whether you are (1) buying at proper quantities, and (2) buying on proper dates. This way, you can determine whether you are making the best use of your purchase dollar.

As an example, if your inventory shows 150,000 standard half-inch nuts and you find your usage in the manual to be only 30,000 annually, then you would want to investigate. Maybe the purchasing clerk made an error in typing the purchase order. The clerk may have typed 150,000 instead of 15,000. The important point here is that the purchase control manual would have intercepted this discrepancy within one to three months, depending on the date of the physical count. This would have given your company time to plan accordingly. Vendors normally allow returns of standard products within six months; so you could have returned the excess product and recovered your money. Otherwise the company would have a five-year supply on hand, as well as five years' shelving costs.

The product purchase control manual has many uses. Most important, it can give immediate reference for making high-profit business decisions. Every industrial and commercial business organization should have this important guide for use in multiple lines of products.

No Purchase Price Controls

Purchase price control in a business organization is essential. Large amounts of cash dollars are lost when company cash operations employees do not know the correct purchase price of products they buy.

This is exactly the situation at my client's company. There was absolutely no price control on wheels; the vendor was in complete control of prices. After extended research in Purchasing, and some help from the vendor on A to E price lists (quantity/break price lists), we found some contracts for a large number of high-use wheels.

In another discovery in my research, I found that the company had a good, qualified second vendor, but that no competitive bids were transacted between the two primary vendors. Each vendor produced a considerable volume of the business, but neither vendor bid against the other. When I compared prices for new orders, I saw that the secondary vendor had outbid the other by $25,000 in cash profits through COM.

The Wheels Quantity/Break Price List

The A to E price schedule used by the vendors of grinding wheels was a basic price list for low-quantity orders. This, in reality, is the normal quantity/break pricing system used for any purchase product. The system represents variations in the quantities purchased and charged— on the basis of quantity. These A-to-E wheels are distinguished from the high-usage wheels, which, for the most part, were on contract. The A to E price list is illustrated below:

Classification	No. wheels purchased	Price
Contract	1,000 or more	$2.25
E	500	$2.50
D	300	$2.82
C	100	$3.03
B	50	$5.30
A	10	$8.71

This format, along with the prices, was put in the vendor's computers. Depending on the quantity charged on the invoice, the computer scanned the format and printed the price alongside the quantity listed.

Cash Recovery Through COM Price Controls

Let's refer back to the 12X.150X3 wheel used to illustrate the inventory control function. You will recall that my client purchased the wheel 12 times in a 15-month period, for an annual turnover rate of 9.6.

Now we'll follow up on the *price* side of this wheel. We were fortunate to have a contract written. The annual requirement of 1,000 wheels was met, and there were three separate contracts written, one for each price increase over the 15-month period.

In the payables department, while researching through the stacks of invoices, I found that only 3 of 12 invoices had correct prices. All the others, which were on contract, carried higher, erroneous prices.

What had caused the overcharges? The vendor's computer had ignored the contract price and charged the "C" bracket price on the A-to-E schedule. Since my client purchased in quantities of 100, the computer had picked up the 100 "C" price on the schedule erroneously. Thus the vendor's computer was at fault and my client had suffered a cash loss of $702.

In retrospect, can we really blame the computer for the mishap? Shouldn't it really reflect human error—garbage in, garbage out? In this example, the answer is an unequivocal yes: we should look into human error. We should investigate the working habits of the vendor's salesperson. Here is a vital subject regarding cash operations management—vendor's advantage (VA). The basic concepts of VA are covered in their entirety in Chapter 8. Here, I refer to VA to emphasize its importance in the cash recovery on a single grinding wheel.

The problem was that the vendor's salesperson did not update the computer to take into account the fact that the 12X.150X3 grinding wheel was a contract wheel and should be priced accordingly. The result was a cash loss of $702, which slipped below the cash management level-line. Following is a billing recap on the wheel:

Cash Recovery Program Benefits

Grinding wheel purchased

Description and size	12X.150X3
Quantity	1,200
Price paid	$3.03
Should have paid	$2.25
Difference in prices	$0.78
Cash recovery/credit memo	$702

Because I had prepared myself with a qualified price base, the vendor had no alternative but to issue a credit memo. My client had earned a cash recovery of $702 through principles applied in his COM program.

In the above example, the grinding wheel had set a pattern for recovery of cash profits in the overall theme of cash operations management. In this company the COM wheel program accumulated more than *$15,500 in cash recovery.* All was received from the same basic approach as was used with the 12×.150×3 wheel. This approach can be practiced in every type of business organization that processes industrial and commercial products.

Systems and Procedures Improvements Through COM Price Controls

Several systems and procedure price problems affected the cash profit areas of the grinding wheel at my client company. In addition to the cash recovery benefits described above, new profit dollars were earned immediately after we implemented improvements in systems and procedures in wheel purchases and inventory control.

Order Discrepancies

The high value of the losses were experienced through low-quantity orders on wheels that were used at a high rate. This caused excessive prices on noncontract wheels, which put the prices in the A and B rather than the D and E categories on the price schedule. As you can see, this increased the price of the product by 100 to 250 percent.

For the basic reason behind the situation described above, we must go back to the machine operator who left his machine to go to the purchasing office to order a dozen wheels at a time— a two-weeks supply instead of a three-months supply. On grinding wheels alone, this procedure cost the company more than $50,000 a year.

Second, the lack of information about usage control resulted in rush orders, on which premium prices were paid. Sam Dixon occasionally ran out of inventory of specific wheels. This was no coincidence; it was an error in purchasing responsibility. Premium prices on rush orders can cost as much as 450 percent over the regular price. It is done unfairly by some vendors, but it *is* done. This type of overcharge is virtually unrecoverable in any company job or cash-recovery program.

The third discrepancy was made in the purchase of special wheels. Specials were bought when a lower-priced, standard wheel would have been sufficient. Sometimes the most complex products are not the best. A grinding wheel of .125 thickness will grind as well as one of .130 thickness, but the .130—only one-thousandth of an inch thicker—is specially made at $4.09 each, whereas the .125-inch-thick wheel is regularly priced at $2.02 each.

Inventory Control

Inflation was always present; prices were escalating in jumps of 20 percent. Buying from the vendor before his abortive increase would have saved my client thousands of dollars in company profits. This is where a good inventory control system pays for itself almost overnight.

Profit-oriented managers are alert in periods of high inflation. When vendors announce price increases, that is the signal to look at your inventory balances and your future cash outlays for purchased materials. If you plan to make purchases soon after the scheduled increase anyway, get your high turnover orders in at the lower prices, then concern yourself with paying for the material later. The important thing is to be in a position to know at any given time how much material or purchase items you will need to make a qualified, educated, cash-profit decision in the future.

A Major Usage-Control Oversight

An overestimate of usage figures during a short-supply economy caused an overorder situation for my grinding wheel client. More than $378,000 in outstanding orders had to be cut back by 71 percent because current inventories would have exceeded a one- to three-year supply.

This may seem inexcusable, but the Purchasing people were not altogether wrong on these purchases. This was during the gasoline and oil shortage of 1974. Since grinding wheels, to a certain extent, have a petroleum base, it was reasonable to believe the supplier's projection of a short supply in 1975.

Purchasing's inclination was to overorder. Thus the company would receive its normal shipment. It backfired. There was no shortage, but the vendor kept sending wheels at the overorder rate of a 3-year supply instead of a 3-month supply.

This is where the purchase control manual comes in. The overflow could be recognized, using the principles outlined in the manual. We put order cancellations through in time to stop the vendor from overcommiting to the vendor's suppliers.

What amounts were involved? Three wheel-purchase commitments of $378,000, less 71 percent ($268,380) in cancellations, equaled a balance of approximately $110,000. This brought the wheel stock back to the normal three months' usage rate.

The saving was in the cost of money. This was a one-year commitment on $268,380 at 12 percent. The orders were stopped, and the value of the interest on shelf cost was saved (the amount was $33,200 in cash-systems improvements times a 3-year stock).

The applicable cash operations management principle here is: be careful of your purchase commitments; they require *follow-up*. The vendor was not about to tell his customers to cut back. His commitments were already figured in their sales plans. It is the Purchasing people who must keep on top of extended-purchase commitments. The product purchase control manual gets the credit for this one; the purchasing and accounting departments had overlooked it.

Implementing Competitive Bids

My grinding wheel client did not try to improve prices by the use of competitive bids. The opportunity was there but not the proper purchase pricing functions.

What is meant by *proper purchase pricing functions?* In this case it means quality, usage, count, and price. First, we need quality vendors; next, we must have an inventory product-by-product control so that we can establish our usage rate and the precise quantity we wish to buy from the vendor. Third is the price at which we can buy the product in the most economical quantity.

My client's employees were not concerned with these purchasing functions. Because the company had no organized purchase plan, competitive bidding was neglected. Sam Dixon's purchase procedures had not grown with the company.

Wheel vendors are not particularly adapted to producing all grinding wheels with the same performance characteristics. As an example, some vendors are proficient at manufacturing small wheels, whereas others are better at large wheels. The purchase-analysis responsibility here was to select the wheels for competitive bidding that could be produced by more than one vendor at high standards. I was successful in getting the company to do this. The purchase of numerous wheels was established according to the principle of competitive bidding.

The wheel's purchase control manual made possible the accurate ordering from vendors; from there on, it was a matter of vendor supply and price. For my client the first time around, the annual cash savings on new bids was approximately $35,000.

Poor Purchase Procedures

While conducting the COM program on grinding wheels for my client, I discovered that there was no organized purchase plan in use. Also, no procedures were written to guide Purchasing in its work. Such shortcomings can prove costly to business organizations.

Poor purchase procedures can be illustrated in numerous ways. A vivid example was the machine operators placing orders directly with the purchasing agent instead of processing requests through the stockroom. Another was low-quantity purchases made on high-usage wheels. Overpurchases were made of low-usage wheels. Excessive prices on vendor invoices were ignored. There was a lack of usage information on a product-by-product basis. These are just a few of the cash-loss idiosyncrasies that accompany poor purchase procedures.

The Big-4 Format of Purchasing

The responsibility of the purchasing agent (PA) in a company is (1) to get the best product on the market (quality), (2) at the best price, (3) at the best usage (count), and (4) on the most timely basis. This job is so important to company cash profits that the PA must be allocated total support to do the job right. The PA cannot be tied down with clerical details, delivery, or materials-handling assignments or any other unrelated business activity that will detract concentration from the four principles listed above, which I call the "Big-4 Format."

When your purchasing agent can stick to this format, the company is getting the greatest use of its purchasing dollar. If the PA varies from this format, financial trouble will soon find its way to the purchasing office.

To succeed in developing the Big-4 Format, the purchasing agent is expected to be among the most proficient of organizers. The PA must use the most basic, the most modern and efficient business forms that will give quick reference on a product-by-product basis. The company must also multiply its investment by providing the PA with up-to-date purchase tools.

Once the PA is established in buying, he or she has taken one of the most demanding dollar responsibilities of any employee in the organization. "One dollar lost in purchasing," the old adage goes, "is worth twelve dollars in sales effort." The PA cannot vary from the purchase path, just as a salesperson cannot vary from the sales format.

The purchasing agent is a decision maker in the broadest financial sense, and should not be asked to stray from the Big-4 Format. The PA's position demands VIP recognition, particularly since the price increases of 200 to 300 percent in 1974. The PA, of course, must carry the credentials to qualify for the responsibilities (common sense more so than a college degree, although a college degree is always welcome in business), but he or she must meet high standards because of the cash-profit risk that the employer is assuming.

Such standards are not all that difficult to find in a purchasing agent. If the PA makes a concentrated effort and is interested in purchasing work, success will likely follow. The PA will need encouragement, just as a salesperson needs—and gets—encouragement. When the PA proves savings of profit dollars through quality Big-4 Format purchases, management should recognize this accomplishment. The accomplishment should be made known among the staff in the office, as well as mentioned in staff meetings. Companies recognize and award the $100,000 salesperson. The time has come to recognize the $100,000 purchasing agent. Why? First, because the purchasing profit dollar is that important to company profits; and second, because it is important to the person—it keeps the PA going.

Sam Dixon's purchase procedures were far from meeting the Big-4 Format standards. Sam perhaps got the best product, and sometimes he got it quickly, but when he did, it was only by chance. He did not use a value-analysis approach to purchasing, nor did he know the best price available or his rate of usage.

As we have seen, Sam's deviation from the Big-4 Format cost his company an abundant amount in cash operations profits. My recommendations for improving purchase procedures were numerous. The two most important procedures are mentioned only briefly here; they are covered in detail in subsequent chapters. They are vendor's advantage (VA) and the part number principle (PNP). The initial steps in procedure improvement here were to provide the purchasing department with a purchase control manual on grinding wheels and to emphasize the use of the Big-Four Format.

No Stockroom Control

How much money and time are you saving as a manager or employee by knowing the exact location of a paper, a product, a tool, or a supply item you need immediately in your work? Multiply these figures by 200, by 400, or even by 3,000 (the number of employees who work in your business organization). You will notice that the statistics can become astronomical in dollars and hours over a period of time.

It was this savings in dollars and hours that my client gained by using the COM program. The reason for this savings was that he had no stockroom controls; to put it simply, he had *no stockroom at at all*. The client failed to control the small inventory products or manufacturing-expense items in his plants. This included grinding wheels products.

When I explained the disastrous inventory control and purchasing situation to the company president, particularly concerning grinding wheels, he acted immediately. Stockroom cages were installed in every plant.

The work done on the new stockrooms was concentrated on vital improvements, for example, a base for inventory control and physical counts, security precautions, and putting a stop to the breakage. Every grinding wheel in the inventory—225 in all—had its place on shelves and was filed under its own identification, or part, number. In front of each stack of wheels on the shelf, in a cellophane pocket, was placed a perpetual-inventory index card that displayed incoming and outgoing items and the current balance for each wheel.

Conscientious, older employees were promoted to work in the storerooms as managers to account for every item that moved in or out of the cage. They were also given the responsibility for ordering wheels through the purchasing office according to a closely monitored principle of inventory control. This took the load off the machine operators, much to their dismay.

There were 120 machines. The price of a grinding wheel ranged from $2 to $25. Even when production people were careful, the loss from breakage alone must have reached $3,000 a year.

Whether the wheels were stolen for other machines or for resale outside the plant, the theft was costly. The employee loses critical production time when forced to steal wheels or other supplies to keep machines operating. The employee is jeopardizing his or her job in stealing for resale. In the case described, the new stockrooms relieved them of the temptation.

What labor-saving benefits were derived by installing stockrooms? There were many. (1) Now employees did not have to search for wheels or supplies; the supplies awaited them in the cage. (2) Employees did not have to go to Purchasing to order wheels; the stock clerk ordered and stocked wheels at the best quantity/break price. (3) Managers did not have to guess at the rate of usage. With a sign-out system in use, the company was now in a position to determine which departments had excess usage or spoilage of products. The figures derived from this system gave usable statistics for the utilization of manufacturing-expense items, as well as telling the company what its cost-accounting needs were. Various expense areas could now be identified. Most important, the statistics revealed which departments and shifts were responsible for negative profits. (4) Physical inventory was improved. The larger the company, the greater the demand for annual financial information.

These benefits are four good reasons why every commercial and industrial organization should have stockroom (or storeroom) facilities.

Once the stockroom was in operation at the grinding-wheel company, it was interesting how other expense items, such as gloves, safety glasses, and tools, decreased in annual costs. One surprising expenditure cutback was of all things, in sweeping compound for the floors. The stuff must have gone home in lunch boxes.

Back-Up Statistics for Wheel's COM Program

There are numerous, important, functional profit areas in a cash operations management program. Numerous areas in the grinding-wheel project have already been discussed, such as inventory control, price and cash control, and order discrepancies. Now let us recap other aspects of this particular COM program, which were not included initially. They are, in a sense, hidden functions that contribute to profits; but they also carry the element of surprise concerning COM profit dollars.

Hidden Profit Functions of COM in Procurement

We will investigate five different subject areas in the grinding-wheels chapter: (1) organizational processing costs; (2) freight costs; (3) staffing your offices to handle cash disbursements as well as staffing other departments; (4) "head chopper" strategies; and (5) sources used to develop the grinding-wheels COM program.

Additional Purchase-Processing Costs

Have you ever sat down and thought about the cost of processing a purchase order through an industrial or commercial organization? By this, I mean every detail: the time, the thought, and the effort required, as well as the cost of the materials and equipment needed to complete a purchase transaction. You have a surprise awaiting you if you have not considered the matter recently. For purposes of increasing profits, let us follow up on some costs involved in cutting a purchase order for processing through the company.

First, assume that Sam Dixon is running the purchasing department. Keep in mind that our purpose is to find the cost of processing a purchased product through a business organization.

Sam made some horrendous errors. A good example is the at-random purchase of grinding wheels. Sometimes Sam cut purchase orders (not releases) for 200 wheels when 1,200 was the amount needed for three months. Thus he processed six PO's when *one* was the proper amount. As it was, he made an additional five purchase orders over a three-month period, or an average of 20 unnecessary PO's written annually on one product. Knowing that the company had 225 wheel applications, times 20 unneeded PO's per application, gives us an astounding hypothetical sum of 4,500 unnecessary PO's written annually. Of course, the sum is absurd; I give it to make a point. It is questionable how "absurd" the figure is; remember that Sam made 12 purchases of a .150 wheel during a 15-month period, when five would have been sufficient. Then there is the certainty of the numerous other products purchased within the company. What do they contribute to additional processing costs? But let's use a hypothetical, conservative figure of 1,500 unnecessary wheel orders processed in Sam Dixon's company.

Seven COM Purchase Order Processing Functions

Now let's go to the next step. Through the process of elimination, basically seven cash-management functions are exercised in processing a purchase order through an industrial or a commercial organization. We will go down the list of functions and attempt to apply a cost factor to each function. While doing this, keep in mind that Sam's company normally processes 4,000 PO's annually. Add to this the 1,500 unnecessary PO's written because of bad purchase procedures. When we have established a cost factor on the seven functions, we will compare it with Sam's 5,500 purchase orders distributed.

The seven COM cost-processing functions involved in putting a purchase order through a business organization are:

1. *Initial analysis of the purchase.* What product are we buying? How much time will go into "purchase information thoughts" to be typed on the purchase order? Here is an example. If you buy a technical product such as a grinding wheel, description and specifications must be listed. This usually takes about three lines on the PO. The quantity, price, date, terms, and delivery and shipping date arrangements must all be entered. Also, the most important money factor—usage and inventory control analysis—must be exercised. Accumulating this information for each product purchased requires the valuable time of a purchasing agent, an executive, a manager, or a clerk, depending on the circumstances of the purchase. Cost: these costs will vary, but let's attempt to be conservative and assume that the above time takes 20 minutes at an average wage of $7.50 per hour, or $2.50 per order.

2. *Typing the purchase order.* Typing the purchase order is not easy, particularly on a multiple form that requires highly technical descriptions. Suppose there is a typing error on a 5-part form, or even worse, on a 14-

part form. I've seen 14-part PO's distributed throughout a company. (The form was hideous. Eventually I had it changed to 8 parts, but it was still an extremely bulky purchase form.) Regardless of the number of parts, they can rob a purchase order form of employee *time* and expensive expertise required to type it fast and accurately. Cost: a good technical typist should cost approximately $4.50 per hour and average 15 minutes in typing a purchase order, or $1.15 per order.

3. *Forms cost.* Have your ever originated an office business form? It requires intense study, new improvement ideas over the past form, interviewing suppliers' salespeople, gathering thoughts from employees in other departments using the form, and so forth. A business form is expensive. The initial cost, as mentioned in number 1, and the printing of the form builds an investment that must be written off in the next few years. Thus, with each purchase of a product, add a fixed cost for a business form. Cost: 25 cents per order.

4. *Mail, phone and transportation costs.* At times it may take several days to put a typed purchase order through the company's system if the system encounters problems. If the system is on computers, it might take five weeks to cut a purchase order. Thus phone calls become part of the purchase transaction.

Phone calls can be a problem, because of the chance of verbal errors, and such errors are costly. Even when the phone is used, a purchase order must still be processed, and that means mailing costs. For one order, a normal mail cost is anticipated, which can be controlled. If Purchasing is ordering too often for the department's usage, however, company mail costs can increase significantly. The same factor applies to transportation costs for bringing ordered materials into your company. Freight costs are covered below; our concern here is with the minimum charge on *unnecessary* orders. Today, such a charge is in the area of $12.50 per order. Cost for mail, phone, etc.: $1.10 per order.

5. *Accounts payable processing costs.* Once in awhile, when you're near an accounts payable desk, you may notice a disgruntled payables clerk, particularly if the clerk is confronted with a new stack of vendor's invoices that just came in the morning's mail.

That clerk knows a great deal of work is needed to process that stack of invoices through the system. Approvals are needed, filing is required, payment process forms must be written and accounting codes entered, checks must be printed via expensive computer time. In addition, routine price and extension checks must be made. The most important task is to verify receipt of the material or service. If there is an error in shipment or some other discrepancy, other employees will become involved, and credit memos and debit memos will have to be followed up.

All these functions are important in protecting the president's or the owners' financial interest in the company. Assigning a cost factor to payables processing is prohibitive. Some payments may take only 10 minutes to process, whereas others can take 2 hours spread over a period of several weeks. Therefore, let's base the payment area on the expected number of purchase orders distributed annually—in this case, 4,000. Cost: using an average wage base for clerks and supervisors of $8,000, plus the cost of forms and computer time, yields a process cost of $2.50 per order.

6. *Receiving department and storage areas.* The position of receiving clerk is another underrated job in business organizations. How many times during the year do you feel, as a manager or an executive, that you are being short shrifted by some of your vendors, and that you are unable to do anything about it? Many times, I'll bet. Why would this happen? Because your receiving clerk was too occupied with responsible work to make reliable counts of shipments arriving at your company's receiving dock. I've experienced the same bitter reactions in many companies; but in my position as a consultant, I have been able to do something about it.

To give an example, I insisted that one of my clients install a floor scale at the receiving dock, because of information I had uncovered about some short shipments of steel. The company followed my advice, and within two days a new $5,000 scale had paid for itself. It turned out that the vendor who had been supplying steel had left some boxes of steel rods lying on its factory floor; those rods should have gone to the customer—my client. It was a periodic occurrence that took cash dollars from my client. On extremely short notice, my client installed floor scales in all the company's other plants—something for steel buyers to remember. The steel company still did not improve its shipping procedures, but my client improved his profits.

In retrospect, the Receiving function is most important in cash operations management. It pays to introduce new, useful concepts in this area. Here are some ideas, which may already have been implemented in your company:

1. Equip your receiving clerk with scales, counting equipment (weight-count scale, lift trucks, etc.).
2. Allocate adequate space to the area—the more space, the more time for counting before the material is trucked to production inventories.
3. When applicable, have production people and stock clerks make counts of materials received. Provide them with forms that they can submit to the payables/purchase system, which will stop payment

of an invoice until discrepancies are accounted for by the people using the material.

4. It is imperative that clerks in Receiving put their counts *in writing* on receiving reports, especially for audit trail purposes, but also for cash savings. Auditing will pay its way on the receiving dock.

Certainly all of this is extra work, but it pays dividends in extra profits. Once your vendors know that you are counting, they will be much more likely to improve their shipping procedures.

The receiving dock is highly susceptible to losses of profit dollars. Treat it with respect regarding security and proper business procedures; and use your common sense. In addition, it would not hurt for the president or other VIPs in the company to review periodically the receiving clerk's job and performance on the loading docks, if only for improvement ideas. The docks are an area where "hustling dollars" could supplement the business education of an eager, profit-oriented executive Cost: savings are big; wages, materials-handling costs, space, etc., are applicable: $7.25 per order.

Did I actually suggest that the company president leave his or her ivory tower and look into trouble areas on the receiving dock? Who is this guy kidding, you might ask.

Let me explain. Company presidents and other top executives do take walks through the production areas of their companies. At least, the effective ones do. They do so for several reasons, all of which are intended to improve cash operations management.

The COM system is designed to detect all the stops in the operations part of a business. When I state that dollars can be found on receiving docks or anywhere else in a business, it is because I have seen firsthand the escape of profit dollars in these areas. If a consultant can spot lost dollars, so can an executive. But executives have more to offer.

When an executive walks through the production plant, that executive is noticed. Employees notice, and morale is lifted. The walk-through carries the message that the executive *cares*. If an executive cares, so will the employees. If you give them half a chance to tell you cost-saving ideas, they will give you a basketful of "profit makers."

7. *Closing the order.* When the management consultant looks at a closed purchase order, he or she wants to see as many notes as possible that will explain what the client received for the cash spent in the purchase transaction. If the price was changed, the change should be written on the face of the PO. If proper quantities were not received or if defective material was returned, written notes are even more important to cash management and recovery. Writing notes is not a normal procedure, but it makes good common business sense to keep yourself and the

employees informed about what alterations have been made on a purchase order or a change order. If a consultant needs it, so do company employees.

Files are another fixed expense in closed purchase orders. Again, if unnecessary orders are processed, here is where they end up. Files are expensive; they take up valuable space in company offices. Both the IRS and outside auditors need them. But even more important, in cash operations management, closed PO files are as valuable as gold. Cost for space, labor, file boxes, etc.: $.50 per order.

The seven points just discussed tell a great deal about how processing costs on a single business form can affect corporation profits. The total dollars represented by the costs of processing a purchase order should be a keen reminder to management people that profit dollars do have escape areas. The estimated cost figures for each processing area, based on 4,000 orders, were as follows:

Purchase Order	Cost per Order
1. Initial analysis	$2.50
2. Typing the PO	1.15
3. Forms	.25
4. Mail, phone, transportation	1.10
5. Accounts payable, EDP	2.50
6. Receiving department	7.25
total processing costs per order	14.75
times 4,000 orders	59,000.00
additional 1,500 excess orders	
minimum freight charges (half rate) @ $6.25	9,375.00
1,500 times $14.75 per order	22,125.00
total annual purchase order processing costs	$90,500.00

(sales volume approx. $16 million)

To summarize, an approximate cost of $59,000 was the average annual price tag for processing purchase orders through my client's $16-million-sales-volume company. This included normal, expected costs when basic control procedures were followed. The base will vary with different kinds of companies; for a basic industrial products company, however, this figure can be considered a good general-cost base.

Under a poor purchase control system such as that described above, additional processing costs can be significant. An additional 1,500 purchase orders (37.5% increase in orders) multiplies the annual processing costs to $31,500—a 53.4% increase. Minimum freight charges were a significant part of this expense. Most of the additional orders were for low-quantity purchases, thus fixed, minimum freight charges were applicable. These small orders could have caught a free ride if they had been shipped with orders involving more than 5,000 pounds. The theory is that it will cost as much for a freight truck to deliver a 30-pound package as it will a 300-pound one, or in thousand-pound multiples.

Here in the Processing cost area is where the purchasing agent must watch controls. Sam Dixon lost his company $31,500 simply because he did not follow up on his Big-4 Format. He did not know what his *usage* was or what he should buy on the most time-efficient basis. All of this adds up to inventory control. Later on, we'll identify this as a loss through the part number principle (PNP).

Additional Freight Costs

It irks me as a management consultant to find my clients paying freight bills at both ends of the company. By this, I mean they are paying incoming freight on purchased goods and outgoing freight on products going to their customers.

The reason for my dismay is twofold: it may not be in the sales price of your product, and it may already be in the purchase price. The additional annual processing costs to pay a freight bill can accumulate to a considerable amount—as illustrated above.

Why should a company be pressed between its vendors and its customers to absorb a half-million dollars a year in freight costs? This question is asked by many of my clients while I am conducting a COM program for their companies. Their answers are nearly always the same: they agree that they should not have to pay freight both ways. But then they drop the subject and change the subject to something more pertinent to their business—perhaps that of the three-martini lunch.

I've seen $80-million-sales companies that did not have the cash to pay a small, wilting vendor $5,000 so that he could keep his payroll intact. Yet these same executives would not lift a finger to help themselves make $100,000 in profits simply by streamlining their company's freight policy.

What happens to a company that has lost control of its freight costs? Profit losses, of course, but we have already discussed that. Business people simply do not consider freight costs important enough to warrant stringent audit procedures, even in the current inflation-riddled economy. Another explanation, I believe, is that management people do not particularly want to tangle with freight companies. It is widely believed that freight companies have a poor reputation. They are heavily involved with labor unions, and the Federal Trade Commission demands payment of freight bills within seven days (look for a change) or it may threaten prosecution. This, understandably, can be a deterrent to getting involved; but it need not be. As far as I can tell, freight company people will do what they are asked. They will ship as instructed, whether prepaid or collect.

So this puts the onus back on industrial and commercial companies. It is they who must set the policies. Sales and purchasing people must draw the line on what freight costs they can absorb and what they can negotiate.

The Need for Rigid Freight Policies

Sales people are profit antagonists when it comes to the peripheral areas of their deals. The weaker salesperson in the field will throw in the freight if it will close the deal on a big package, and this *hits the profit nail on the head*. The salesperson goes back to the sales manager with the results, which may be no results at all. The sale may be good volume, and it could pay a lot of overhead. Generally, though, big packages carry a penalty of low price. By the time the discounts are in and the commissions are out, the profit margin is dependent on the freight and the pallets that hold the order in the shipping department. If the customer does not pay for both, the salesperson has made a deal for a long-term profit loss.

This is often the case. Profit has little chance in some business transactions. Suppose the salesperson mentioned above had Sam Dixon for a purchasing agent. The combination could demolish a good profit enterprise.

The point here is that a company must set rigid policies on payment of freight costs. If it is sophisticated, these policies can be set on the profit margin from the computer. If a manual system is used, the value of the sale should be the criterion. Whichever is the case, sales management must stick to the guideline. They must also have a grip on cost controls and know when product costs are out of line.

The same applies to people in Purchasing. The purchasing agent's strongest freight-saving device is the term *Destination*. The PA must apply for destination terms, both on the written quote and on the purchase order, to make sure that the cost of freight is included in the vendor's price. This is the PA's cash management base. Thus, if the PA is charged for freight erroneously, there is recourse—in writing—for cash recovery. In addition, destination freight will eliminate the cost of processing a check for the freight bill.

Staffing Your Offices in Accounts Payable

Let us picture ourselves walking into an actual accounts payable office of a large service company on Chicago's Michigan Avenue.

Now let us look at the staff who handle the cash disbursements of this company. The company employs a staff of eight. Four are college graduates, three are working toward degrees, and there is a secretary. The accounts payable manager of this staff has in-depth business experience, say, ten years, and is considered to have a prominent position on the company's accounting management staff.

The point here is that college-level people handle Payables. Five employees process invoices, purchase orders, and receipts from the A-to-Z payables files. Their payment vouchers are processed to a supervisor who audits the work and searches the vouchers for timeliness of payment, price, receipts, cash discounts, 30-day terms, freight costs, and proper purchase followup.

Next the supervisor sends the vouchers to two payment specialists in the front office. One specialist audits the paperwork a second time and examines it for additional purchase values. When these audit checks are made, the vouchers are sent to the payment officer. After final adjustments, the checks are printed by the computer, which sends the printed checks back to the payment officer and an assistant for further audit. At this point the payments receive a final check from the accounts-payable manager and are sent to the vendors.

Essentially, this accounts payable office is given responsible, qualified employees, because the cash-disbursements function is considered an important part of the company's profit structure. A final note: *few* cash losses ever slipped through this payables system.

Now let's compare the staff described above with that of another company. The A-to-Z files were handled by two people fresh out of high school and one Payables woman with a year's experience. Two outside plants had their own people to handle a 50-percent payables function; the remainder was done at the home office. The payables supervisor, a woman experienced in payables, was allocated no time to supervise the three workers under her or to check their work. Practically all of her time was spent making decisions about what payment amounts should be distributed and in dealing with vendor problems caused by bad procedures on the part of employees. The next plateau was the accounting manager, who wanted to have nothing to do with accounts payable.

In essence, this company ignored the control principles (established through the COM program) of its payables function and lost more than $1 million per year in cash profits because of it.

Management people in business organizations must draw a parallel between the two employee policies followed by these two companies. There must be a reason why some companies use college-trained people to process their money. One reason, obviously, is the $1 million in lost profits. The question is, What is wrong with the companies under weaker control? It would seem that management in these companies would notice such obvious losses. If duplicate payments were made on invoices, and if obvious price errors were ignored, one would think that management would want to do something about it. Strangely enough, some top managers today do not recognize the impact of million-dollar losses in their companies even when their companies have gross profits of only 2 to 4 percent per year.

As an example, I recall an incident when some company accountants discontinued my services at a time when my COM program was recovering more than $460 per hour for the client. Break that down on an individual basis, and it totals $1 million or more in cash recovery per individual per year, and $10,000 in monthly interest income thereafter.

I overheard the accounting manager of this company talking to his accountants one day about stopping my consultant services (which to date has not been renewed): "I've never known anyone to *hang on* and milk a company so long. Man, that consultant was here for months."

This accounting manager had overlooked something that had occurred only three months earlier. He had come begging for me to find him more cash profits to put on his March 31 fiscal, year-end statement.

Within a week, I returned more than $50,000 in cash to him. My total contribution to his statement profits that year were in excess of $450,000 (for four months' COM work). The accounting manager had forgotten these contributions by July 31. By then he had reported a year-end profit to the owners and stockholders and was off the hook. But the consultant, he said, was "hanging on."

Eventually such incompetent managers are found out. This one got in via the "political route," by becoming a friend of a nonprofit-oriented (but entirely accounting-oriented) financial vice-president. The problem was that the owners of the company lost millions of dollars in profits before they could do something about such managers.

A cash operations management program is one way to locate deficient systems operated by mediocre (or worse) managers. All of the facts turned up by the COM program are based on in-depth analysis. A separate COM program, one promoted by top management people, can slip through the various barriers that conceal organizational profits.

Educated, qualified employees will pay for themselves many times over in the cash operations management areas of business organizations. Go for the college graduate in the disbursements and receivables cash functions of your company. Then pay good wages to get that graduate some well-qualified employees. It can be worth a million dollars.

"Head-Chopper" Strategies

Now that we are on the subject of company employees, let us talk about those who are fired. The "head-chopper" tactics of some industrial and commercial organizations will cost those organizations much in the way of profits in their cash operations management areas. I am referring to the decisions made at the top—the headquarters of conglomerates. For example, at the decision level, how many instances have you seen of a telegram notice such as the following?

> Fire ten percent of your employees, across the board, in every department, NOW. This will stop an immediate cash outflow (payroll expenditure), which will give us emergency cash funds to pay off financial obligations at the corporate level.

This is not to be taken lightly. I've seen it happen. As a matter of fact, it can be a common occurrence in low-profit companies that are in financial distress. The tactic does not cure expense problems, however; even worse, it increases immediate cash losses and profit losses. Therefore it appears to have no purpose.

Perhaps over a period of time, some fat has accumulated in various company departments. But to take a flat 10 percent away from each department, without a cash operations employee time-study analysis that would identify each employee's contribution, is a poor business decision.

This tactic is more critical in cash operations areas than in other departments, because *cash* is what management needs. Practically every department has cash operations employees. Suppose, for example, that a 10-percent order is issued that involves a purchasing agent who is getting a $500,000 price decrease on a blanket order about to close in two weeks. Some companies depend on only one employee to handle negotiations on this size transaction. Or perhaps this is the only purchasing agent left in the office. The manager would not likely take on such detailed work. A certain profit loss would occur, probably the full half-million dollars.

Suppose the 10-percent cuts out a payables clerk. Maybe there were two of them. Firing one would increase the work load of the other person by 100 percent. Assuming that there was enough work for two people, something would have to be given up. That something would probably be price checks, since that is the most time-consuming job of the payables clerk and the easiest to cover for. Among some of my client companies, this procedural weakness alone would lead to million-dollar profit losses.

Another example is firing an insurance clerk in Personnel. This may be the only person in the company who knows how to find the statistics that allow for a $15,000 credit on health insurance premiums from the prior year. If the clerk is fired, the credit for the $15,000 dies, too. Because no other finance-oriented person is employed in the personnel office, no one is left to pick up on insurance matters.

These functions, as well as numerous others, are often overlooked when an irrational head-chopping business decision is made from a far-off corporate office. More often than not, these cash operations jobs and functions require beefing up rather than cutting back. This has been particularly true since the spurt of inflation in 1974.

Sources of Information

It is important to find good sources of information when conducting a COM program. The program is so profit-oriented that even a modest grasp of the program will probably bring cash profits up front. Thus, if you can locate good sources of cash operations information, you should receive excellent dollar returns from your COM program.

In the COM program for the user of grinding wheels, the procedures employed were so bad that we could not expect much from the sources of information. The reason why procedures are bad and dollars are lost is usually that a company keeps poor records for its business systems. To achieve success in this program, a positive approach is needed, just as it is in most success stories. You make do with what is available. And this brings us back to the grinding-wheels program and our first source of information.

The Index Card File

The grinding-wheels purchase index card file became an important tool in determining the pattern in which the company was purchasing grinding wheels. The fact it existed at all was a coincidence. The file was not used for any particular purpose, perhaps only as a minor quantity reference by the production department. The company president must have stopped in the office years before to inquire about grinding wheels. Therefore, Sam Dixon long since decided he'd better keep a card on the purchase and prices of wheels.

Dixon, as I mentioned, was meticulous about procedures. Fortunately for his employer, he did a fairly meticulous job on the cards. They were accurate and complete enough to be a valuable secondary reference for purchase quantities and pricing history. The numbers on the cards could be referenced (by PO numbers) to paid invoices in Accounting, which is always the ultimate reference in cash operations.

Something worth repeating about the cards was that I could not find anyone in the company who needed them frequently as a business reference. Keeping the cards updated was something Sam Dixon had done for years without a particular purpose. Then one day a consultant came along, and at last, to everyone's surprise, the cards were needed. The point here is that people in business can spend many hours on work that is never used, referred to, or even seen by the people who make decisions. This waste is, indeed, costly.

What was the importance of the index file in the COM program? First, it offered a history of quantities purchased. Second, it was highly noticeable—from purchase to purchase—that prices on individual wheel deliveries varied, regardless of the quantities involved. This consistently appeared on each card (for each wheel purchased); thus it was obvious that the probability of a significant pricing problem existed if, in fact, the same prices were paid on payables invoices. The prices given on the cards, it was determined later, were copied from the vendor's invoices. Sam Dixon's price base—the index cards—was no price base at all. He did not use price lists as a basis for prices on the cards.

The quantities listed on the cards were helpful in showing us the varying quantities shipped.

Purchase Orders for Grinding Wheels

Purchase orders are normally used by a consultant seeking information from which to determine if there is good control of purchases. Purchase orders are useful only if effective PO forms are developed and used. This was not done in the case described.

Examples of the use of good procedures in processing purchase orders is difficult to find in business today, although it is not impossible if a purchasing department is properly staffed with capable people. No doubt about it: capable people in Purchasing will pay off in the form of high cash profits.

In the case of the grinding-wheels client, there were numerous discrepancies that prevented the company's purchase order from qualifying as a primary cash reference source. The most obvious were:

1. Purchase orders were not prenumbered. Numbers were handwritten in the top right-hand corner. This curtails control over purchasing documentation, in that a purchase order could be issued, processed through the system for payment, and then destroyed, along with

the receiving ticket, freight bill, and paid invoice. This provides—
also on an equal scale—the opportunity of preparing an altered
purchase order to cover losses caused by incompetence.

2. Prices were not entered on the orders. Price lists from vendors were
not available for reference.

3. Low-quantity purchases were made on high-quantity purchase
wheels.

4. Lack of control of procedures caused a need for rush orders, on
which premium prices were paid.

5. Payment and freight terms, discounts, and special agreements were
not written on purchase orders.

Accounts Payable Reference

The accounts-payable function in Accounting was somewhat better
organized. A well-maintained file was kept on paid checks, with
corresponding invoices attached. This provided a good basic source of
information for the COM program. The only problem for expediency
values was the transition to a manual function once the check was
returned from the computer. No cumulative cost records were maintained
by the computer.

Accounting's only payment responsibility, other than processing the
invoice to the computer, was to match the receiving ticket with the proper invoice, and attach it. Payables had no pricing responsibilities.

It was frightening to know that the financial people in this company
had no vendor pricing responsibilities. This meant the only pricing
function on vendor's invoices was the responsibility of Purchasing. Since
that department had no specific documentation on grinding-wheel
prices—or on any other material purchase items, for that matter—the
floodgates were wide open for cash losses. This explains why Sam Dixon
did not need price lists for his 225 wheels: no one ever checked or audited
his prices.

Price Lists and Contracts

The most useful source of information was the most difficult to find, in
terms of availability. I wanted valid vendor price lists on the wheels, both
for prior years and for current. If they were not available in Sam Dixon's
office, I would have to try the more difficult source—the vendor.

As luck would have it, in an in-depth interview with Sam, I unearthed
some signed contracts buried in a lower desk drawer. Interviewing Sam
was like pulling teeth, but the result was important; the contracts proved
useful. They offered special long-term prices for high-volume purchases

of individual wheels. This was the key to negotiating cash for bad prices charged by the vendor—if that turned out to be the case.

The contracts were simple documents: one page written separately for each grinding wheel purchased in high volume. Each time a price increase came through, the vendor sent another set of contracts to the production manager and the purchasing agent's office. The contracts did not cover every wheel purchased, of course, but additional contracts could be obtained from the vendor once the base price had been established.

Sam had not bothered to use the contracts. He was never audited by Accounting. Therefore why would he worry about prices and controls? Apparently management had never questioned the purchasing practices of their long-time employee. On the other hand, how could they? When you work next to someone for 15 years, how can you accuse that person of doing a poor job? Management should never become involved in such a position. Managers should establish stringent procedures and systems covering these matters. When payables are established in Purchasing, systems and procedures should follow up with periodic audits of pricing and receiving.

Grinding-Wheels COM Program Benefits

Cash Recovery	Amount
Prices on overcharges	$15,500
Inventory control	
lower prices on competitive bids	10,490
inventory reduction/cost of money	33,200
purchases before price increases	5,430
total cash recovery	$64,620
Systems and Procedure Losses	
Order discrepancies (A–E prices)	$50,000
Lower prices on competitive bids	25,000
Inventory control improvements	27,000
Storage facilities	3,000
Processing cost improvements	31,500
total lost cash/future savings	$136,500
total first-year benefits on wheels COM program	$201,120

Recap on COM Benefits

Two COM benefits were derived from the grinding-wheels program: cash recovery, and systems and procedures benefits.

The cash recovery benefits were developed from four COM concepts, three introduced for the first time in this book. The first was from (1) price overcharges caused by an overzealous vendor and a not-so-active purchasing agent (vendor's advantage). The recovery was $15,500 cash. The other cash benefits were: (2) acquiring lower prices through competitive bids on future orders—the amount, $10,490; (3) inventories were reduced by using the product control manual. The amount of cash saved was $33,200 annually. A 20-percent increase in the price of the wheels occurred on November 30. The product control manual had been completed in time to tell us that we would need $27,150 worth of wheels two weeks after the increase. I told the president: "You'll have to buy these wheels in the next two weeks anyway, John. Let's order them now and pay the invoices on the regular terms after the two-week period."

"Can we do that, Jerry?" The President was about to pay his bills.

"With your triple-A credit rating, John, "you have nothing to be concerned about. In addition, you'll make an additional $5,400."

"Go ahead, Jerry. Let's make the money." I was the first person in 15 years in a position to make him this "cash profit" offer—through *product-by-product* inventory control. He liked making manufacturing expense decisions on the solid ground of cash operations management.

The total benefit was $64,620 recovered, for a short-term profit-improvement program—below the cash management level-line. The systems and procedures gains, though not surprising, revealed even greater benefits. The order discrepancies on A-to-E prices showed the greatest profit improvement for the coming year—$50,000. Lower prices on forecasted purchases over 12 months, due to the acquisition of competitive bids, reached $25,000. Basic inventory-control improvements were estimated at $27,000. Storage facility improvements in breakage alone should be $3,000. Overall processing cost improvements, because of the installation of these controls, is expected to increase profits by $31,500. The total improvements on the above system were estimated at $136,500 in additional annual profits.

Another important COM note here is that the new profits and ideas will encourage and compound more of the same. Labor-saving ideas about the stockroom, the product control manual, and improved procedures are not included in the above figures. The grinding-wheels program is an excellent illustration of "cash operations management" in action.

In Figure 6.2 are shown the important cash-profit features of the grinding-wheels program.

Figure 6.2 Cash profit features of the grinding-wheels program

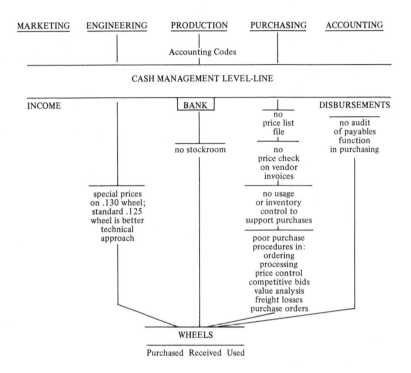

Summary

The cash operations management approach to finding new profits generally begins with interviews in the various departments of a company. The company's employees know their company better than anyone else, and they do not mind talking about making improvements.

Various tools are needed to conduct a COM profit program. Problems must be viewed from different perspectives. Vendors' checks, the product control manual, product inventory stock reports, vendors' price lists, and so on are a few of the tools needed.

Employee responsibilities play a big part in COM. For instance, the Big-4 Format of purchasing is vital to maintaining organizational profits. Stockroom control, monitoring processing and freight costs, staffing cash control departments, and utilizing product-by-product control—all should play an important role in your company's financial success.

Questions on Chapter 6

PURCHASING AND INVENTORY CONTROL

1. Does your company buy multiline products? For use in manufacturing? For resale?
2. What kind of detail records does your company keep on multiline-purchased products? Does it maintain index card files? Inventory usage, computer printouts by part number? A stockroom, perpetual-inventory record?
3. What person or department uses the product records?
4. What system or procedures do your production people follow in requisitioning total product purchases? Through the stockroom? Production manager? Purchasing agent?
5. Are effective procedures followed in completing purchase orders sent to the vendor? Are prices typed on the order? Are directions for delivery, dates and terms complete? Are part numbers used? Are the POs prenumbered?
6. Are low-quantity purchases made on high-volume products?
7. Are numerous rush orders processed on which premium prices are paid?
8. Which department handles the vendor invoice price-check function in your company?
9. If the price-check function is performed by Purchasing, is a periodic accounting audit conducted?
10. Do you anticipate a multiline purchase problem in your company? Do you see a COM program as a solution?
11. Do you feel you have a management profit problem in your company? Do you see a COM program as a solution for this problem?
12. Do your purchasing agents follow the Big-4 Format when procuring multiline and high-usage products?
13. Are your PAs expending additional processing costs by not ordering enough products on each order? Are they eliminating as many unnecessary purchase orders as possible?
14. Are your PAs overordering, thus wasting cash on shelving costs?
15. What basic records are employed to determine the relationship of usage to product purchases?
16. Do you have extremely high inventory balances on some of your purchased items? Why are these balances high?
17. Are your purchasing agents given the most up-to-date purchase tools for conducting business in their offices—for example, forms, EDP support, product manuals and guides?

18. What evidence is there that your PAs are getting competitive bids on their purchases?
19. What is the cost factor in your company for the additional processing costs of unnecessary purchase orders?
20. Do you have a bad usage situation that has led to a process-cost problem?
21. Is your receiving dock a large enough depot to allow an accurate count of everything received before moving it to the departments?
22. Are you satisfied with the counting procedures used by your receiving clerk? Do you feel money could be saved by improving the receiving area?
23. Is your receiving area equipped to make this a profitable area (such equipment as floor scales, weight-count scales, and lift trucks)?
24. What is your estimate of the cost of processing purchase orders through your company?
25. Is your company paying premium freight charges on products transferred through the company?
26. Are you being double-charged for freight? In your invoice prices as well as on freight bills?
27. Has your company run a freight-cost analysis to determine what process costs amount to in this functional area?
28. How many multiline products does your company have to which the purchase control manual could be applied?
29. Have your purchasing people been instructed to ask vendors why such increases for the vendor's product have occurred? Or why the vendor's product(s) now carry such a high price?

7. The Part Number Principle

You will recall my conversation with the president of the grinding-wheels company about buying wheels ahead of schedule. "You'll have to buy the wheels in two weeks anyway," I told him. "Let's buy them now to beat the increase and make $5,400 on the decision."

Let us elaborate on the significance of buying ahead of schedule. There must be more involved than merely the $5,400, although that sum alone is good enough reason. Why was I the first person in 15 years to suggest such a procedure?

The answer is the *part number principle* (PNP). PNP is the one-on-one concept, product-by-product theory that forms the basis of multiple, increased profits in industry and commerce. Just minutes after I had worked out the part number principle for my grinding-wheels client, I had the company president on the phone, saying "Let's act now; your money is at stake—$5,400."

What is this principle of business profits, this Aladdin's lamp of good business fortune? Why hadn't my client already used PNP? If PNP is so effective, why hasn't it long since been written up in the business manuals?

The truth is, for years, it has been written about, discussed, and used. Companies use it every day in their routine production operations—if they have good controls on these operations. The principle has been hidden and suppressed under the comprehensive title *inventory control.*

How can it be so important? Let us take another example, one from the same client company. Recall, in Chapter 6, the overestimate of usage figures during a short-supply economy that caused an overorder situation on grinding wheels for my client? More than $378,000 in outstanding orders had to be cut back by 71 percent because current inventories would have exceeded a one- to three-year supply. *The overextension was discovered principles using* PNP. The cost-of-money saving alone was $32,000 in shelf-cost interest, plus the savings in storage space, since space is valuable in company plants. The PNP picked up this loss early, even before the vendor overextended with its own suppliers. The values of this transaction were high in terms of cash profits. Those values were made possible by PNP.

What Is the Part Number Principle?

What is the purpose of PNP? Why is it called the "part number principle"? How can PNP be used to discover money problems early, before losses occur? Let us break the term down by answering these questions in everyday language.

The part number principle is more easily identified as an *advanced combination* of inventory control and product-usage control. The theory behind it has to do with the one-on-one, product-by-product, part-number approach that will follow a purchased or manufactured part through your business operation.

When you need a particular part or product in production or distribution, you buy or manufacture the part or product and enter it in your inventory. *How many* parts you buy or make, and *when* you buy or make them, is determined by the PNP.

The PNP is, in theory, a fairly simple business function. To make it work, however, requires an organizer with initiative. A complete PNP company program is not easy to accomplish; but it is, indeed, a profitable business goal—a goal that, in my opinion, belongs in an organization's standard procedures.

What Is the Purpose of PNP?

The purpose of PNP in business is comparable to that of the minicomputer in today's data processing market. It will do jobs that operators of large computers find uneconomical to process. The same principle applies here. PNP is a smaller program, manual or computerized, that will become part of your control program more quickly and easily than you could expect from your present, bulky, inventory-control program.

The basic PNP idea is to know what you need in inventory sooner and with more accuracy than what you have experienced in your present inventory-control system. To know these timely, pertinent facts is virtually a guarantee of increased profits through cash operations management.

How Does PNP Discover the Problem Early?

Let us take an example from a client who had a production plant in Texas. A purchasing clerk in the home office, in Cincinnati, made a typing error on a purchase order. Instead of typing 15,000 bolts (3" × ½"), the clerk typed 150,000 bolts in the quantity column. The typographical error slipped through the normal purchase audit procedures (which were almost nonexistent), and the vendor promptly shipped the 150,000 bolts.

This was an overorder of $3,375 in unwanted bolts. It increased the stock on hand to a 27-month level. Three months later I introduced my COM program into the company. Through routine consultant steps in the program, I conducted a PNP test on some products in the inventory by using the product control manual. The overorder of 135,000 bolts fell out as a PNP overstock problem.

Steps Toward PNP

Because PNP is an important part of cash operations management, let us backtrack to see what was done to locate PNP problems, using the 3½-inch bolt above as an example.

My first step was to review the computer's inventory printout of purchased parts. This printout showed multiline-inventory products with balances greater than $1,000, which I recorded in the purchase control manual. Inevitably, the 3″×½″ bolt showed up as an item to be tested in the manual (bolts were classified as a multiline product, based on different sizes, value, and volume used).

Next I scanned the "supply on hand" area of *Inventory Status*. The 27-month stock of bolts stood out. It became a suspect part—one of many—in my PNP analysis.

The background work done on the bolt included the usual checkpoints:

1. *Purchase history.* Gleaned from paid invoices, purchase orders, perpetual inventory cards, or sometimes even filed index cards that Sam Dixon maintained for the grinding wheels. In the present case, we used quantities from computer purchase-usage records and backed them up with paid invoices. This information reinforced our belief that usage on this bolt was much lower than that detected by the purchase order for 150,000 bolts.

2. *Current usage.* What quantities had production people pulled from stock since the 150,000 purchase? Usage turned out to be the same as the prior year—5,000 per month.

3. *A definite discrepancy.* The proven current usage, compared to the usage before the 150,000 purchase, revealed a definite overpurchase of the part.

Action Taken on the Purchase

My next step was to visit the purchasing department. It was there, when the purchase requisition was matched with the purchase order, that the 150,000-quantity discrepancy was revealed.

My first phone call was to the vendor. Then I called the plant's production manager in Texas. "I didn't know where they were coming from, we had so many of them," the production manager answered. "I tried to send some to the other plants, but they wouldn't take them. I knew it was our fault, once I checked our copy of the purchase order down here. I just figured we were stuck with them."

This is a usual reaction of plant employees. These employees will give honest answers in such situations. The production manager in Texas had nothing to hide; the error wasn't his responsibility. The point here is that plant employees at times need help in making operations decisions. Every employee, at times, can use outside ideas.

"On the contrary," I assured him. "You don't have to be stuck with them. I've just been on the line with the vendor. Since these bolts are a fairly standard item, we can still return our overstock bolts, or whatever we don't need. But we have to do it within three months. The vendor has a written six-month return policy in our purchase agreements on standard items."

The production manager appreciated the news. The parts were shipped back to the vendor and $3,375 in cash was returned to my client. The part number principle had again proved its value in new cash-profit benefits.

The discovery of the PNP problem in this particular company was not the ultimate in timeliness, but it was early enough to prevent large money losses on the transaction. If my PNP program had been conducted in the company earlier, obviously the problem would have been detected earlier. The point here is that PNP will discover problems early, before big losses occur, using the same basic approach as that described above.

What is the First Step in Discovering PNP Profits?

I have just shown how PNP can uncover profit problems hidden in inventory control records. Our PNP approach offered immediate profits in cash and cost of money by (1) returning parts or products to vendors for refunds (bolts), (2) making a 71-percent cutback in purchases (wheels), (3) buying ahead of price increases (wheels). All of the above were immediate cash-profit adjustments discovered by use of the part number principle. PNP is not limited to the three items listed. There are numerous ways in which the PNP can be used to increase profits. In the above analysis we determined *how many* parts should have been purchased and *when* they should have been purchased. It is a simple approach, one that is focused on the rate of usage of a product in inventory.

In my opinion, companies do not emphasize sufficiently the usage rate of inventory control. Employees in this company had available the same information I used to determine the error in the purchase of 150,000 bolts; *but they did not use that information.*

Why didn't they? As I see it, this PNP analysis work just was not included in the employees' work responsibilities. It was not in their procedures. These profits will not spring from a magic formula; to retrieve PNP dollars, companies must allocate employee time.

I could mention numerous examples illustrating the importance of the part number principle and how it can locate new cash profits for business organizations, if that would clarify the definition of PNP. In a later chapter, I explain an almost unbelievable example of how only one multiline product—production envelopes—caused more than 165 separate PNP problems similar to the bolt problem just described.

The point here, however, is that each of the above problems required hours of work—on my part or that of an employee. But these hours of work paid big dividends—which is a good reason why employee hours should be allocated to PNP.

These problems were handled one step at a time, on a product-by-product basis. The PNP "work route" was direct, just as is illustrated in the bolt problem. The first step was inventory history and led to the product control manual, to a PNP usage analysis, and finally to new profits.

Other Advantages of PNP

Intercepts Changes Quickly

The PNP approach is an addition to inventory control in an organization. It can intercept changes in inventory status quickly, faster than the normal control system, which may produce statistics only once a month. When a PNP analysis is conducted, several essential inventory facts are exposed:

Current balance of inventory. It takes only moments to make a physical count of an in-plant product. Division plant employees do not mind contributing an occasional count either, over the phone, if it adds profit dollars.

Purchases outstanding. What quantities are presently on order? Check the purchase order file. Keep your eyes open for other facts that can help in this review.

Current and past usage. A purchase history of past purchases and the dates of the purchases can help determine annual and monthly usage of the product. This is total purchases divided by the number of months it took to consume the product. These figures could be more difficult to find. If the computer history of inventories, purchasing, or vendor payments is not available, a manual search must be made. Although vendor invoices and past purchase orders become the primary sources, perpetual inventory cards or even simple index cards can help provide a purchase history.

Price history. Hopefully, a price history can be acquired from vendor price lists; if not, vendor invoices become the primary source.

The information indicated above is collected and transferred to a product control manual, which then provides all the facts needed to analyze the movement of a product. When future changes occur on the account, they should be entered and compared with past statistics. This is where PNP profits show up. It is also where bad statistics and profit losses fall out of the system.

It is here—in the transfer of inventory-status information—that future opportunities lie. To update the product control manual is an elementary task and can be done quickly, for purchase forecasts or for abrupt changes in usage. All changes in future inventory statistics will jump out of this system promptly—in the form of new cash profits.

Offers Current Statistics for Lower Inventory Costs

The PNP approach will give each specific, high-value product in the inventory a separate identity. It will provide the current usage and give a count status for fast reference. The product, under an assigned part number, will have undergone an individual current analysis on a: (1) physical inventory count; (2) purchase review before releasing a purchase order; and (3) analysis on excess activity in steps 1 and 2.

When this information is published, the company purchasing people will have more useful facts about their product than what their monthly inventory control records tell them. Why? Because these monthly records include statistics for a complete inventory and because they may already be out of date.

Obviously, to compile statistics for the complete inventory will require more time than that taken by the PNP approach, which will analyze only high-value, multiline products. The monthly information feed-in source is slower, even on a computer. This is particularly true when information sources are bad or when the computer has scheduling problems. By the time monthly figures are out, they are probably outdated for PNP purposes. Inventory figures can become outdated in two or three days, sometimes in hours, if price increases, purchases, or production figures become eratic. A number of dramatic things can happen between the time the purchase order is sent and the delivery of the material.

Considering the above information, we are on solid ground when we say that PNP will assist the purchasing agent in making decisions. The PNP statistics provide necessary, current information for maintaining lower inventory costs.

Summary

The part number principle can also be used as a tool for recovering new profits through cash operations management. When applied in the business organization, its principle makes possible the in-depth search for operational materials and values that can make employee work easier.

In order to make the most of the president's dollar, it is imperative that vital people in the organization, in marketing as well as purchasing, get the most current inventory information possible on a product-by-product basis. This principle applies whether one product or five thousand products are involved, whether a manual system or an extensive computer system is used. *PNP must be applied*—after the regular inventory control or usage analysis is processed.

8. Vendor's Advantage: A Profit Loser in Purchasing

Not all companies take advantage of their customers, and not all salespeople take advantage of their customers. Some companies and some salespeople, however, do take advantage of their "sleeping" customers. They do it with such ease that the customer seldom knows that profits are being lost. The customer continues to believe that he or she is getting a real bargain.

As a management consultant, I have recovered hundreds of thousands of lost dollars for my clients through what I call "vendor's advantage." On a single multiline product I've seen as much as 30 percent of a vendor's invoices billed at the wrong price. You guessed it: all of the invoices were overcharges.

What, exactly, is "vendor's advantage" (VA)? In what form does it appear in business organizations? Who is responsible? These questions were asked by curious victims of VA.

I consider the practice of vendor's advantage somewhat dated. It began, with I believe, the advent of massive computers that seem to chew up money. Later we will investigate why computers have had such an impact in VA.

The term "vendor's advantage" means that vendors have a financial advantage over their customers in business transactions. It can be honest, so far as vendors are concerned. The responsibility for the loss rests solely with the customer's cash operations management controls.

What Basic Elements Are Found in Vendor's Advantage?

1. The advantage originates when a vendor charges a higher price for a product than what was negotiated at the time of purchase.
2. The advantage continues when the vendor's company representative or salesperson, voluntarily or involuntarily, decides not to make an adjustment that would reactivate lower contract prices.
3. The advantage is completed if the customer does not follow the principles of good buying, good cash disbursements, or good inventory control (PNP).

An example may serve to illustrate the above. Recall the case of the grinding wheels. Sam Dixon did not do his job fully. He did not set up a chronological price list for controlling the prices he should pay for each grinding wheel. He ignored the price and inventory control principles simply by dropping his price contracts in a desk drawer, never referring to them again.

What Sam did not know was that the vendor's salesperson knew that he had ignored the PNP. Since it was the salesperson's responsibility to forward new contract prices and changes to the vendor's computers, this put Sam Dixon and his company in a precarious situation. The company's entire pricing structure for grinding wheels was based on the vendor's trust and salesperson's need to make a commission. Which do you think won out? Correct. My grinding-wheels client became a victim of vendor's advantage to the tune of $160,000 per year.

The Steel Company Case

In another client case, I analyzed a questionable sales procedure used by a well-known steel company near Pittsburgh, Pennsylvania. Because this company did not want its competitors to know that it was selling steel for less than the national suggested exchange price, it offered my client a regulated credit-discount plan. In this case the invoices were billed properly by the computers, but on a monthly basis the steel company issued a credit to my client that reduced the billed price by a marked percentage.

The interesting problem that I found when I arrived on the scene, however, was that the discount structure was so complicated that, at the end of the month, my client did not understand how much credit he was entitled to. He was so delighted that he was receiving credits that amounted to $25,000 a month that he did not bother to check whether the discount was in the correct amount. My analysis showed that, on this question alone, my client had lost more than $29,000 in one six-month discount period. This had been going on for two years, and until my COM program discovered the loss, both parties were satisfied that the transaction was complete and accurate and that it had been handled properly. Again, it was a case of vendor's advantage.

Why Wasn't the Error Caught in Accounting?

The steel company credits appeared correct after a cursory accounting check, but the accountant could not give much time to this cash-credit project and merely assumed that the vendor was correct. It is strange that some accountants will work all month to put out a general ledger and financial statements (a report) but find it difficult to allocate one hour for a financial analysis that could earn the company an additional $29,000 in profits.

On the other hand, putting out a financial statement and handling tax profits is also important. Perhaps that is all an accountant should do in an organization. That is the accountant's responsibility. We will go into this subject at greater length below; meanwhile, my feeling was that my client should turn over the *profit* projects to an analyst—to a profit-oriented employee. This client certainly needed such a person, if for no other reason than that $29,000.

In short, a monthly financial analysis should have been conducted on the steel company's account. My client had no one in any department with the necessary profit instincts and curiosity to put in this profit project. Accountants were only accountants—perhaps good accountants but still not "profit people." There is a difference between being an accountant and a profit person. The other company employees were all tied down to the functional business problems they were hired to do. Thus, a large opening had been created for vendor's advantage, with the customer becoming the "victim." *The vendor was holding the money.*

What Happens in a System Victimized by Vendor's Advantage?

Accounts Payable

Normally management people expect their accounts-payable employees to run a routine check on prices charged on vendor invoices. And usually this is correct. Normal business circumstances, however, sometimes become disarrayed and confused in payables offices.

In some instances, company employees avoid intruding in the details of clerical work when they have no procedures to guide them. Many good employees who do want to get into detail work are sometimes not given the time or the opportunity to follow up on such profitable work—for example, checking to see whether a credit memo was received for materials returned to the vendor.

Initially, then, vendor's advantage may experience a breakdown in accounts-payable procedures. I have found that it is not altogether the fault of the employees; management, too, can cause VA problems, by not providing systems and procedures with which to follow up on unfinished profit-loss work.

Purchasing

What happens when the responsibility for pricing rests with the purchasing department? Again, employee attitudes and goals, as well as moral support from management, affect to a large extent the success of a company's cash operations management procedures in purchasing.

Purchasing managers and agents must be alert when a vendor's-advantage problem arises. Their most important function is to bring themselves up-to-date on the various components of the purchase (the Big-4 Format again). These components are quantity, price breaks, bids, methods of price control, vendor's price lists, and a purchase control manual. Purchasing managers and agents must use any practical method to acquire knowledge that will give immediate, accurate reference to the price to be paid for parts or products.

Examples that show the importance of the above are, first, the case of the grinding wheels. The company's routine pricing procedures were nonexistent. Sam Dixon simply did not conduct a systematic price check on the 225 different grinding wheels the company used.

Second, in another company, a vendor billed my client according to eight different price lists covering discounts for six plants scattered across the country. The probability of a purchasing or a payables clerk finding a correct price in this structure was virtually nonexistent. Yet the company's purchasing agent spent hours negotiating low contract prices with this vendor, to no avail. His company had no one (it had an abominable payables department) to make sure the lower prices were paid. Inevitably, higher prices were paid, and more than $1 million annually was lost by a company with a $50-million sales volume simply because its controls were lax and its vendor's computers had an add-on system that resulted in overcharging on invoices.

The Customer's Rights

Whatever happened to that admirable American business term, *the customer is always right*? It is high time that the business people of the United States start to reemphasize this term and put it back in everyday business life. And I am not fooled by the term *seller's market*, because, as far as I am concerned, we are in a "pirate's market." But that is another subject.

The point here is important, a detail that can go wrong in the system. It is the customer's right to question vendors' prices. Management should insist that employees question vendors if their prices are abnormally high. Ask the vendor directly why such a high price is being demanded for a product. If the marketing service clerk's response is inadequate, go directly to the president of the organization. Sometimes even corporate presidents are surprised at what their employees charge for companies' products. If you happen to be a big customer, the company president is bound to be concerned.

If the vendor fails to give a satisfactory answer, investigate getting a lower price for the same product from one of the vendor's competitors. Explain to the vendor that the vendor's price gouging is contributing to the erosion of the dollar today. Most products are not worth the price charged. It is not demand that has caused prices to rise since 1974—it is greed.

Vendor's Advantage and Its Cure

Vendor's advantage eventually will occur in your organization. Thus it is important to discover it and then do something about it. This raises the question, How can I determine whether VA exists in my organization?

Vendor's advantage has to do with a built-in price-elevation policy on vendors' computers. That is a major approach to discovering VA. Your vendor will never charge you a lower price. Your price will always be higher or exactly correct, depending on whether you have contract or blanket purchase orders and whether your vendor's computers are up-to-date with pricing data.

Let me explain by going back to the quantity-break system discussed in Chapter 6. The A–E price scale for grinding wheels is illustrated, along with contract prices. We will use another size grinding wheel to illustrate this price policy, size 12X.625X5. The vendor's plan is as follows:

Classification	No. wheels purchased	Price
plan (contract)	500	$12.50
E	125	16.75
D	50	18.98
C	25	21.34
B	10	24.84
A	5	32.19

Let's say our company purchases more than 500 wheels of the above size during the next year. That means the company qualifies for the contract price. Now let's assume that the vendor's salesperson failed to put our contract price on the computer and that 25 wheels are released for shipment. What's going to happen on the billed invoice?

Of course our company will be billed at the "C" level, or $21.34 per wheel. If the salesperson had renewed our contract on the computer, we would have been billed at $12.50 each. This is a difference of $221 on one invoice, a 41.4-percent markup. If all 500 wheels had been shipped on the 25-release base (hopefully not, for PNP and for price and process cost purposes), the additional price would be $4,420 *in lost profits.*

Now let's assume that our vendor's computer is programmed to bill its customers according to the Vendor Price List. It will never bill a lower price on a shipment of 25, for example, because the "C" price (for 25) is locked into the computer program. The only way a lower price can be charged is to release greater quantities at the "D" and "E" levels. Keep in mind that quantities dominate the program; the A-E classification does not. Classification can control the print-out price. But, again, only if the salesperson or marketing service clerk instructs the computer to do so.

The next step is to understand what the payables and purchasing clerks see when they are ready to price check the invoice. They are handed the vendor's price list, which contains the figures in the Vendor's Price List. First, they look at the price and quantity on the invoice. They see the quantity—25—and the price—$21.34. When they compare these figures with the price list, not surprisingly, the figures match. There's no question about it: since the price matches, they can pay the invoice. The payment is processed, and the company becomes a victim of VA in the amount of $221. The employee or employees do not consider the possibility of a contract price.

Who's Responsible for Vendor's Advantage?

The Clerk

The question now is, Who is responsible? The payables clerk was correct, that the price for the quantity shipped matched the price on the list. The purchasing clerk was correct (on the purchase order), that the quantity and corresponding price were based on the same price list. Neither clerk would have known about a contract price on this product unless that clerk was informed—by a signal, a code, or a routine price submission *from the purchasing agent.*

This is where the initial breakdown of a system occurs. This section of the system, however, should have procedures written so that clerks are alerted to contracts and lower prices on certain parts. The problem here, of course, is that more clerical detail work is generated, and that increases employee time on particular jobs. In spite of the problems involved, we also must see the *profit potential.* The question now is, Would your company change systems and procedures on the old system in order to *improve* profits by 23 to 41.4 percent on bad purchases?

Hold on for a minute, though. We've just let the brunt of the problem fall on the purchasing agent. Let's get the agent's side before we draw too many conclusions.

The Purchasing Agent

We have talked about a vendor who provides one product line with 225 applications. This purchasing agent may be responsible for 200 vendors. If the PA doesn't have a good system and set of procedures to incorporate, there are 200 possible loose ends to tie together continuously. On the other hand, the PA may have already recognized the contract problem, solved and presented it to the purchasing manager or a vice-president. The solution could be buried in a stack of papers the purchasing manager or vice-president will get to later. But there is a strong probability that this will never happen. The PA did the right thing, however, in getting a lower contract price.

As we have seen, even the purchasing agent may not be responsible. It depends on the organizational structure of the system, and in every organization, management runs the system—hopefully with the cooperation of its employees.

The Vendor

Let us get back to a more likely culprit: the vendor. The purchasing agent depended on the vendor's salesperson to put the contract price into the computer. If this has happened, there would be no problem.

Whether the vendor's salesperson dodged putting the price in the computer intentionally is a good question. However, if we intend to make more profits for our company, *we must not depend on others to do our work for us.* This, in reality, is the basic cause of vendor's advantage.

The Salesperson

Now, in getting the problem off the purchasing agent's back, the vendor's salesperson is the scapegoat. But let us keep up front the possibility that the vendor's salesperson is honest. Granted, salespeople, can be tempted; anyone can, and some do, make mistakes. A generation or two ago, salesmen (they were invariably men then) had shady reputations as peddlers. Today that reputation has changed, and so have the services and assistance they can offer to their customers.

An elderly salesman I questioned about VA told me one day: "Jerry, I just can't keep up with the paperwork today. I'm covered up so much in paperwork that I can't make calls on my customers. We use long sales forms to feed our computers information. Those forms take so much time that I can't get everything done. In the old days, all I had to do was call on my customers and sell them. Today I lose sales because I'm sitting at a desk—inside—feeding information to computers. My company loses."

The man had a point. His abilities lay in showing his company's products to prospective buyers. He was good at his job; he was successful. When he was pushed into deskwork (as large conglomerates and others tend to do with their employees), his talents were wasted— and so were his company's profits.

The Computer

Now let us look at this from another angle. Suppose that the salesperson submitted the correct price to the computer. The salesperson did the job correctly, but the information *did not take.* This can happen; computers have many programming problems, both electrical and mechanical. To some extent, this removes the human element; it also opens the gates of profit loss to mechanical failure. How early this can be detected and corrected will determine the extent of losses. But what methods are available for dealing with these dollar problems?

Good people in Payables and Purchasing, along with good procedures, can catch the losses. An alert salesperson can also catch the problem, if he or she initiates honest adjustments. If neither party catches the error, the *vendor,* of course, will profit from the discrepancy—because the vendor holds the advantage.

What Is the Cure for Vendor's Advantage?

The multiple functions of a COM program is the best cure for vendors advantage. If we apply cash operations management skills to VA, improved systems and procedures can be developed.

The best, overall cure is to establish an airtight system, with error-proof procedures, that will tie up the loose ends of controlling cash in your organization. If your company COM system exposes severe cash losses as a result of VA, PNP, payables, billing, or receivables profit problems, or as a result of any cash-related problems, you must improve your cash-management systems and procedures.

If your company does not have the employee talent available, you should seek professional help in the field. The cost of implementing new systems and procedures should be nominal, because your COM program has directed you to the problem areas and *paid* you "lost dollars" in cash recovery to find them. The systems professionals have only to submit forms, improve the basic systems, and write the procedures to instruct your employees in the proper methods to use in doing their work.

Summary

The explanation of vendor's advantage, as described above, lies in its simplicity. The computer approach is used here because of the computer's effect on the cash operations management area today. It is in the computers that the greatest volume of VA losses will occur in an organization. This is by no means the only route vendors may use to take advantage of their customers. The shortage credits from the steel company in Pittsburgh is one example.

There will always be numerous ways in which vendors can profit from their customers. The idea here is that cash operations management employees must be imaginative in making cash decisions.

9. Boxes, Wastebaskets, and Profits

The chain-reaction profit error in a company is by far the most interesting loser to be found in industrial and commercial business organizations. It is interesting that one bad function can cause a good function or functions, to go sour. Functions may even be segregated, having no relationship to any other part of a business, yet profit dollars are still lost in the segregated areas.

Who, for example, would believe that new corrugated boxes in inventory at the far end of the plant could lead to a profit loss of added labor costs in the maintenance department at the opposite end of the plant? This is a strange combination; as ridiculous as it sounds, though, this was a part of a chain-reaction profit problem in one of my client's production plants.

Cash Losses on the Factory Floor

While walking through a plastics stamping department one morning, I was temporarily blocked by some wastebaskets that were cluttering the aisle between the machines. As I was moving them aside, my arm accidentally caught a jagged edge of a wastebasket. I got my arm and tattered shirtsleeve free. Then I caught a glimpse of what it was: a steel staple protruding from a box flap. The staple was intended to attach the flaps of the corrugated box together at the top, to make the box higher so it could hold more plastic scraps. On this box, however, a flap had torn loose and the staple jutted out from a flap.

I couldn't be sure what grasped my attention most here, the blood flowing down my arm or the discovery of a business profit problem. I stopped and took a good look at what was in front of me. Several questions flashed across my mind. Why were wastebaskets stapled together for use in a production department? Why were new corrugated cartons used as wastebaskets? What was their turnover rate? There must have been 50 or more on the factory floor at any given time. Why not use a heavy-duty plastic wastebasket instead of corrugated cartons? The next thing I had to do was answer these questions and determine what additional costs resulted from using the boxes.

The "Wastebaskets" Interview

I was interested first in getting some background on the use of staples in the flaps. A closer look at the corrugated cartons revealed that the company was using two to three dozen staples on each carton.

"The staples aren't holding," the stockroom manager said. "That's why they use so many. These plastic pieces are heavy. They break through the flaps. It's even common for the pieces to break through the seams in the box."

"What do you figure is the life of one of these wastebaskets?" I asked.

"Two days, at the most. Not more than that, and sometimes less. By the time they go back and forth from the recycler a few times, they're ragged and beaten. That's when the trouble starts."

"What do you mean—'trouble'?"

"The boxes get so chewed up, the staples fall out."

"That's *trouble?*"

"If you call broken knives, maintenance labor, and production downtime caused by recycle back-up a problem, then we have trouble. Don't you agree?"

I nodded my head in agreement and listened as the manager explained the details of the problem. Then I made my way over to the boxes inventory area. There I took the part number from the wastebasket boxes, as well as the name of the box manufacturer. Box companies are required, through industry regulation, to put their company name and the test weight of the box on the outside.

My next stop was at the stapling machine. The staple manufacturer's name was on each role of staple wire. I wrote down the length of wire on each roll for future reference and took a staple that hung from a nearby wastebasket flap as a sample. Now I was ready to go to the accounting department to make an analysis and get some cost comparisons from the cash disbursements records.

The Cash-Dollar Analysis

The method used to determine what costs are involved in a function occurring out on a factory floor can be complicated. The depth of this analysis depends on its purpose.

Our purpose in this chapter is to identify cash losses in what seems to be a faulty production expense operation and to determine the most economical method for stopping the losses. We will call this our "cash-dollar method." If we were to determine the cost on a production operation, such as building a "standard cost" for producing a product, we would expect to get into in-depth analysis to achieve our purpose. Both methods, however, would give us measurable costs to work with.

In this instance, my reason for going to Accounting was to determine the cash-dollar costs of using corrugated cartons as disposable wastebaskets. My approach was to evaluate the cost of materials and estimate the labor costs absorbed in the use of the disposable wastebaskets. This cost, on an annual basis, would be compared with the alternative—a heavy-duty plastic wastebasket.

To establish our goal, we first determine our cost for the heavy-duty plastic wastebasket. This was fairly simple. I turned in a requisition to the purchasing manager and awaited his reply.

The basket required was large—approximately 3 by 3 by 3 feet. But it was a basic, standard size that would help keep the price down. A quantity of 100 was quoted at $7.50 per basket. A basket would be fitted under each of 40 stamping machines. I estimated a six-month supply at this rate of usage. The annual cost for the heavy-duty plastic wastebasket would be $750.

The Analysis

Developing the plan I determined the known cost of materials used in providing wastebaskets. I also investigated costs in other cash-expenditure areas, including labor.

The Cartons

I took a conservative number of boxes—4,200—as the annual usage. This figure was based on 30 boxes used every two days instead of the predicted 50.

The perpetual-inventory cards in Accounting recorded up to 7,800 in purchases during the past year. But actual packaging usage could not have exceeded 2,000 boxes.

The vendors' invoices listed a price of $1.78 per carton, which was identified as a standard, 200#test, double-wall, corrugated container supplied by a major company in the fiber-box industry. After accumulating these facts, I determined that the 4,200 cartons were costing my client approximately $7,500 a year.

The Staples

Wouldn't it be predictable that staples would be the key to the company's chain-reaction profit-loss problem? This was the key to future problems. Let's follow the route of the staples from the production stamping department to other parts of the company. The wastebaskets were placed beneath the stamping machines. These machines punched out plastic roll products and converted them into small, die-cut sheets that were designed for various consumer applications. When the rolls are stamped, die-cut pieces of scrap fall through an opening in the machine into the wastebasket below. The plastic pieces in the wastebaskets are dumped into a recycle machine to be chopped in small, pellet-sized pieces. They are then resold to the plastics supplier as recycled material. If this process moves smoothly, it can be profitable.

But what if a "clinker" such as a staple falls into the works? This is just what happened. When the corrugated wastebaskets were pulled out from under the machines and put on a pallet, considerable strain was placed on the box as well as on the staples containing the box flaps. Most of the time, in moving the boxes, employees would pull on the flaps.

Eventually the strain taxed the holding ability of the staples so much that they separated from the boxes. The punched holes would become so worn that the staples dangled from the box. It was at this stage that the box was hung over the recycle machine. The plastic contents would *push* the dangling staple off the box flaps into the churning knives of the machine.

The "Recycle Machine"

If you've never tested the resiliency of an industrial steel staple, you may be in for a surprise. They are tough; they won't snap. The most you may get them to do is bend. Now imagine that over a period of time, several of these staples fall into the knives of the recycle machine.

The knives in the recycle machine are built for endurance. Here, they were tempered from cold, raw steel and ground to a half-inch edge from a five-eighths-inch plate 4 inches wide and 18 inches long. A set of 4 knives revolves off a heavy-duty hub. The blades strike a half-inch-thick cylinder screen with half-inch holes. It was these holes that forced the plastic pieces into pellets as the knives swept over them. It was also these holes that caught the twisted staples and jammed them against the speeding knives.

The result of the knives hitting the staples was chipped edges on the blades. The resiliency of the staple knocked off the edges piece by piece. Eventually, after four to six weeks of abuse, on the average, the knives had to be reground on the blades, which was done in the maintenance department. Sometimes, if the chips were bad enough, overhaul of a machine had to be done after only two weeks.

Labor Costs

Overhauling the recycle machine was difficult and costly. But can you understand the task taking two full days of a mechanic's and a machinist's time? That was the time allocated for this job. To remove the knives from the machine took a mechanic two and a half hours. Once the knives were removed, they were taken across the factory to Maintenance.

Sharpening the knives was a precision job to be handled by precision tools. All the chips had to be ground out of the knives at precisely the same angle, which could mean a half-inch or more through solid tempered steel. These blades could be on the grinding machine for 12 to 16 hours, under the supervision of a skilled but expensive machinist. The annual cost of sharpening knives, in work hours in the maintenance department alone, was estimated at $5,200.

In retrospect, I recognized other areas of labor costs in this wastebasket project hidden on the plant floor. Following are some of the more important ones.

1. The maintenance department was constantly backlogged with repair jobs. This normally meant that production machines were down. When production lines were down, production employees stood around with nothing to do. I'm sure the lines were given priority, but they might not have gone down if repair crews had been able to do needed preventive maintenance on the machines. Instead, they were fooling around with staples and wastebaskets.
2. Because a machine was down 6 to 10 times per year, the labor required to dismantle the recycle machine and replace the knives when the knives were returned from Maintenance was a considerable added expense.
3. The "staple and box worker" wracked up numerous hours of undisclosed labor every day. The worker's function practically turned into a separate production operation. Imagine how much work was involved in punching 150,000 staples into the flaps of large, bulky, corrugated boxes. More than 4,000 boxes were pulled from inventory, stapled on all sides, up to 36 times, transported to the stamping department, and processed through the plastic-recycle operation.
4. The recycle-machine operator also had problems with the staples. The management people held this operator accountable for dropping the staples into the machine. The operator, of course, could not prevent the staples from dropping into the machine; there were too many of them. It was necessary, however, to slow feed the machine to catch as many staples as possible. The added operational cost here was absurd, but so was the reason for the slow-feed operation.

Wastebaskets COM Program Benefits

System and Procedures Losses	Amount
Purchases	
cartons	$7,500
staples	950
knives (three sets annually)	900
tools	1,750
Labor	
maintenance department	5,200
basket-and-staple employee	1,500
recycle department additional labor	1,200
total disposable-wastebasket costs	$19,200

As we've seen again, unnecessary labor and materials costs needlessly find their way into a business organization. The estimated additional cost for labor in the above operations exceeded $7,900 annually.

When I searched closely for a reason why this company failed to eliminate these added costs, I found that no manager or employee really wanted to do anything about the losses. No one took the initiative to change the wastebaskets or to improve the obviously high cost of labor. These needless profit losses had led to something as trivial as a staple and a box.

Summary

This company's chain-reaction profit error became a $19,200 problem. Problems as serious as this will eat away at cash dollars, day by day, practically unnoticed in the regular workday. If they accumulate from department to department, from plant to plant, they can become major annual cash-dollar problems.

The point I want to make here is that you should anticipate chain-reaction errors happening in *your* company. Your job as a profit person should be to recognize those errors and take steps to stop the resultant loss of profits as early as possible.

Not every chain-reaction error will be equally traumatic, however. This kind of business error, as are most profit-improvement malfunctions, is exposed because of indifference to normal business procedures and practices. If something appears out of the ordinary, run an analysis and compare statistics from one year to the next. Your results may pay off in dividends—to yourself and to your stockholders.

Questions on Chapter 9

1. Have you considered the areas in your own company that may be subject to a chain-reaction profit error?
2. Are there any functions in your production department that you would review for possible change? In other departments?
3. Have you asked your plant employees if they have noticed any current problems that could lead to profit losses?
4. Do your maintenance department people do work that they consider a wasted expense?
5. Does your cost accounting department have total factory expenses accumulated for items on file?
6. Do standard-cost build-ups include all materials and labor on questionable items on the factory floor?
7. Would it cost less to purchase items presently listed under manufacturing expenses?
8. Have you checked the maintenance department's hourly log for extraneous jobs that seem unusual for manufacturing?

10. Envelopes Galore on the Floor: Cash Control in Purchasing

Three of us were sitting on the veranda of the local country club on a warm, beautiful Friday afternoon in August. We had just completed a round of golf and were relaxing, sipping some cool drinks. It was one of those special summer days that come only once in a great while in midwest America. Our view included the plush, green 18th fairway. Member's wives and guests were sitting at other tables chatting about their golf scores.

We had just settled up our fairway debts when the subject arose. "It wasn't this nice back in those days at the plant when you were digging into the envelope inventories, was it, Jerry?" Bill Buskey asked. Bill was general manager of a division of one of my client companies.

"That's for sure, Bill," I answered. "You know that's what brought the three of us together—that envelope problem." I pointed to the man next to me. "John was the sales rep on that program." John Farnsworth, now with his own distributing business, was the third member of our threesome. Here we were some five years later still enjoying a business and personal relationship.

"I'll bet you don't run into many of those, Jerry," John commented. "That was really some gem, that envelope problem."

It surprised me that he remembered it that well. On the other hand, he was the key person to get us out of that dilemma. John understood the quantity-price principle involved in the envelope purchase. Because he did, he could get this account and keep it. He was able to see our problem as a whole, which is why, I'm sure, his distribution business is successful today.

"In my business, John," I continued, "I see many problems similar to that one; but I must say that I'll always remember the envelope program, probably because of the number of business principles involved."

Ordinarily we would not have gone into the envelope subject; it just came up easily. Anyway, it offered me a good opportunity to pull another case history out of my file on cash operations management.

The Envelope Purchase Problem

My first insight into the envelope problem came when I stopped by Josh Brady's purchasing office. It was a small-to-medium-sized company with about $12 million in annual sales. But the company was growing by leaps and bounds. My reason for stopping in Purchasing was to ask about some paid invoices for envelopes. No receiving tickets or back-up information were attached to the vouchers.

"Those are for old envelopes we couldn't use," Josh answered briskly. "They're over two years old, as you may have noticed. We just wrote them off. Told 'em to throw them away."

"Whoa, whoa," I interrupted. "You told *who* to throw *what* away? Are you telling me we're paying $7,155 for envelopes, here on these invoices, envelopes we have never seen—and will never see?"

"Well, yes, you might say that." They're no good to us, so why would we have them shipped here?"

I could have given him several reasons. The fact that we had just paid for them would be the first and foremost. My client had laid out $7,155 in four invoices to pay for production envelopes his company would never use. The cash-control concept here was, to say the least, at odds with accepted business standards. How long had this been going on, I wondered. I was about to find out.

"Could you answer a question for me? If this envelope company manufactured the envelopes for you two years ago, why didn't you take delivery on them and use them then, at the time of the purchase?"

"That's where we got them, Mr. Sinn. We're saving money because Afway [an envelope company that supplied Harco] keeps our envelopes on their shelves until we need them. That saves us inventory space, and we don't have to pay for them till they're delivered."

What an understatement. I walk into the company purchasing office holding $7,155 in cash losses on two-year-old envelopes, never seen or delivered, and the purchasing manager tells me he's making money on them in shelf costs. It was clear that my next assignment was to investigate my client's envelope purchases.

The Cash Operations Analysis Approach

In cash operations analysis work, the consultant must first be certain that the subject of the analysis warrants value and the time needed to make it. That was my first step in the envelope COM program at Harco Company, my new client. In the past five years Harco's envelope purchases had increased by 40 percent over each prior year. Some of the increase seemed suspect, as we will see. One surprising fact, however, was an increase of 163 percent in purchase dollars over the past year. The main reason for this was the start-up of a new plant. Soon that new plant would double Harco's production capacity. The past year's increase brought the total for envelope purchases to approximately $100,000 annually—a good round figure for our base.

Another good figure was that the company stocked and used more than 80 different combinations of envelopes in its production process. These were small envelopes, ranging in size from 2 inches in width to 7 inches in height. Imagine the difficulty of managing the inventory of these multiline products. The envelopes were produced in varying colors, sizes, quantities, styles, weights, paper, and, most important, for varying uses. In addition, each envelope required artwork, type, zincs, and plates. Some 3,500 purchase combinations and decisions were required to supply Harco with envelopes each year. Inventory control would be a massive undertaking. The overriding question was, Who was in charge of this job at Harco?

I wasted no time getting into figures on the envelopes in stock at the Afway Envelope Company, our problem vendor. In my years as a consultant I've seen some bad business controls, but in terms of COM systems and procedures, this one was atrocious. It was not the dollar volume so much as it was the total percentages of the dollar discrepancies that was bad. True, the money was significant, especially considering that this was a company with a sales volume of $12 million. My approach to the envelope problem was to get the answers to four pertinent questions:

1. Why had my client paid for envelopes he did not receive?
2. Who conducted inventory control in the company?
3. How sound were the purchase controls on the envelopes? Would price alone be an important factor here? (If you have a purchasing agent who believes money is being made when it is actually being thrown away, on a scale of $7,155 worth of products, you must have a purchase-control problem.)
4. What was wrong with Harco's facilities for storing envelopes? How did this factor fit into paying for undelivered, obsolete envelopes?

We would find out.

Functions of the Cash Operations Management System

Because cash is the subject of this book, let's first find out why Harco paid cash for products it never received.

My first job was to go after the "bird in hand": the four invoices worth $7,155, with nothing to show for them. A couple of cash-operations principles had already been ignored on these invoices. Now I wanted to learn whether other procedures were also out of line. Here is my analysis of what took place concerning the four invoices:

Amount of Invoice

(1) $3,875.62   Purchased 250,000, although Harco already had 150,000 in stock at the vendor's plant. Usage was 100,000 per year. The 250,000 was never scrapped; no proof of delivery ever turned up. Another order for 250,000 was placed 15 months later. TOTAL LOSS.

(2) 1,259.20   Ordered 5,000, paid for overshipment of 14,000. Had 9,500 become obsolescent. TOTAL LOSS.

(3) 1,086.85   Ordered 70,000; should have ordered 25,000. Total obsolescence of 45,000 envelopes. Oversold by salespeople. TOTAL LOSS.

(4)   933.98   Oversold 50,000 ordered by salesperson. Had 30,000 in stock, with a usage of 15,000 per year, which changed into a usage rate of 4,000 per year. This ended up as a 20-year supply stored on the vendor's shelf. TOTAL LOSS.

Facts of the purchases:

All were purchased early in 1972.

All were paid in September 1973.

All were held at the vendor's plant for 13 to 18 months.

All were scrapped because of obsolescence after 2 years.

All were tagged with increases of 11 to 50 percent in an economy with an inflation rate of 2 to 3 percent.

This information constituted some important reminders of how *not* to impose purchase and inventory controls. Two COM facts stood out as exceptions. First, my client—Harco—had excercised extremely poor purchase procedures. The client had allowed the vendor to control inventory counts. In addition, prices appear to have been neglected. Second, Harco accepted bad advice from the vendor's salesperson. These were extreme cash losses for this type of business transaction. The loss was a 100-percent loss on a $7,155 purchase, something that should never happen in business systems.

How Do Envelope COM Problems Affect the System?

Let us search further for an answer and try to find out why Harco paid cash for something that was never delivered. What was wrong in this purchase system?

In observing the situation, it became obvious that inventory control was a major problem. Also, purchasing and pricing were factors of concern. But how much of the blame should be placed on my client, Harco? Was this a management problem in the system? Was it an explicit case of vendor's advantage? Or was it a purchasing agent doing a poor job or not doing it at all?

I needed more background on the subject. Listed below are some additional discrepancies in the envelope purchase system that were uncovered. New orders were placed ahead of prior orders. On some products the salesperson had *three orders in process at the same time.* Here is an illustration of how it was done on envelope #B-2½×4½ (usage was approximately 30,000 per year):

Purchase order no.	Date	Amount ordered	Amount shipped	In stock as of 6/75
5310	5/72	50,000	51,500	17,000
1240	1/73	30,000	32,260	31,000
2083	3/73	25,000	31,500	5,500
1246	1/74	75,000	37,500	28,500
total stock as of June 1975			152,760	81,500

In June 1975 the stock of this particular envelope stood at 81,500. The May 1972 order still had a balance of 17,000 at the vendor's plant. The January 1973 order was never used. Two months later, the salesperson ordered another 25,000, which represented a 2½-year inventory balance. In addition, another 37,500 were yet to be delivered on the last purchase order—number 1246.

This was clearly a double-barreled combination of vendor's advantage and purchasing incompetence. The vendor's salesperson actually compounded the problem by telling the purchasing agent that inventories were low. The PA, not knowing the true count, duly sent purchase orders as requested.

It was out-and-out negligence on the part of Purchasing. Purchasing people should know what inventories are kept by a vendor. Yet, in this case, Purchasing allowed the vendor to handle inventory control. Purchasing had plenty of warning—even from Accounting—that things were going wrong. When you pay for complete orders that are already obsolete, something has gone awry in your organization. In addition, Harco experienced out-of-stock situations at its outside production plants. How did it happen? Such situations were a clear signal that something was wrong in inventory or production control. The employees of the organization were not meeting important responsibilities.

This imbalance of systems and procedures led to a wide variety of cash profit-loss transactions at Harco. Here are additional examples of things that had gone wrong:

1. Product E-1. A new order for 30,000 went through when the vendor had 25,000 in stock at its plant. Salespeople oversold. Total loss: $704.

2. Product E-2. Ordered 5,000 but 13,000 were shipped (and accepted), resulting in an overshipment in excess of 160 percent. Complete overshipment still on Harco's shelves three years later. Obsolete. Total loss: $518.

3. Product DA-1. The vendor shipped an eight-year supply although Harco had a three-year supply on hand. The salesperson oversold. Total loss: $412.

4. Product B-1. An order for 50,000 was placed although the vendor had 43,000 in stock at its plant (enough for 18 months). Salesperson oversold. Total loss: $1,429.

5. Product B-2. An order for 35,000 was placed although the vendor had 22,000 in stock at its own plant, enough for two years. Mistake: the salesperson did not know they were in stock, and the purchasing agent had no record of shipments against the order. Total loss: $764.

6. Product Gold-1. An order for 50,000 was placed although 28,000 had been in stock at Harco's plant for three years. Usage was 6,000 per year; had 76,000 in stock. A 13-year supply on hand. Total loss: $1,203.

7. Product T-1. A shipment of 38,000 was received, although 3,000 should have been the lowest order accepted. Purchasing agent did not know the usage. A 26-year supply. Total loss: $1,148.

This list continued on and on, accounting for three years of bad business. There were more than 165 discrepancies in items similar to those listed above, *and all caused cash-profit losses.* Harco's management knew that the company had some problems in this area, but they had not realized their extent. The total of the above was staggering in terms of business statistics: total cash losses—$42,000 (over three years), or 35.4% of envelope purchases for the same period. The blunders that caused the deficiencies were:

Overorders by salespeople
Overshipments
Extreme price deficiencies
Purchase errors
VA—salesperson's vendor's advantage
Complete disregard for inventory control by Harco

The Harco management people were stunned by this report. It was difficult for them to accept the fact that they had thrown away 35.4% of purchased materials on one of their multiline products. What kind of system was being used here? What were the statistics on the other purchased products? They were thinking about such matters for the first time. I had raised the prospect of profits, long dormant in their minds.

Steps Toward Discovering Profits

What had I, the consultant, done to recover these statistics? I had taken several steps to determine the cash value represented by the losses. When I sat down and thought about the $7,155 loss on the paid invoices, I saw that I needed to draw some lines to separate the problem. What I learned led me to two distinct conclusions: (1) The vendor had played a large part in controlling the count of the envelope stock. Harco's purchasing agent, without exception, should have devised his own count-control system for envelope purchases. This, however, is easier said than done when 3,500 different purchase combinations of one multiline product are involved. The PA must have known that money was being lost and should have asked for help from management. If he could not originate a successful purchase system (purchase control guide), then management should have found inside or outside assistance to establish a program. There was a three-year delay in making the decision, but management finally did make it; they introduced the cash operations management system. (2) The Harco purchasing agent allowed the vendor freedom to mark up prices, which meant that the PA had no gauge for measuring stock, size, color, or quantity—all of which were needed to determine envelope values. Again, the PA should have asked for help; an envelope price control schedule was needed.

The value of these envelopes had to be divided among color of ink, color of paper, weight of paper, size, order quantity, date of shipment, terms, and so on. Devising a schedule that would cover all this was complicated. In fact, we discovered that it had never been done before, particularly by the envelope vendor who had done business with us on this project.

I designed just such a schedule for Harco. It may not always be necessary to bring in a consultant to design a price purchase schedule, but in this case, it worked. Prices charged for large orders and those for small ones were coordinated. No longer did the small-quantity orders cost more than the large orders, which had until now been common at Harco.

This is where John Farnsworth's company, mentioned at the beginning of this chapter, came in. John recognized the value of adapting to the new price schedule. He had built a good envelope-distribution business since that time, largely attributable, I think, to the price-schedule concept that I suggested.

Review

Once the criteria discussed above (concerning the vendor controlling the count and having the freedom to mark up prices) were established, I was in a position to take steps that would help uncover the reasons for the envelope cash losses. Now we had to determine how big the losses were and what loophole in systems and procedures had made them possible. Also, we still hoped to achieve a cash recovery using the COM program. Let us follow the steps through the Harco Company.

Five Steps in the Cash Analysis

1. *Review the Harco envelope stock.* I needed a physical review, as well as a physical count of the envelopes on the shelves at Harco. These shelves were a disaster. Nothing, it seemed, was in its place. Here are some of the problems:

(a) The envelopes were stacked in cubicles 4 feet by 4 feet by 12 feet high. At least three square feet of each cubicle was open space.

(b) Each envelope had a separate purchase part number. It would have made sense to stack the boxes by part number sequence so production people could go directly to the envelope needed on the line. But it was physically impossible for employees to do this, because nothing was in order. Thus production people used valuable line time searching for envelopes.

(c) Envelopes were spread all over one end of the plant—in different rooms, along walls, on floors, even hidden in nooks and crannies. Apparently, some employees did not trust Purchasing to keep them supplied.

(d) Obsolete and seldom used envelopes occupied 60 percent of the primary storage area. Heavily used envelopes were put in inconvenient areas and stacked on the highest shelves. A ladder was needed to reach them, which deprived the production line of still more time.

(e) I easily understood why Harco had envelope "stock-outs." Envelopes were stored on the dirtiest, dustiest shelves in a dark corner of the assembly plant. Amid confusion, on a manual system, an employee would find it difficult to know even if one of 80 envelopes was out of stock.

2. *Identify envelopes by part number and classification.* We used purchasing and payables documents to establish an identification-part-number base for the envelopes. This would be the basis for forming an envelope purchase guide, which, in time, would control usage, prices, purchase quantities, and inventory for each of the 80 envelopes purchased.

3. *Establish current inventory counts on in-stock items.* Briefly, this was a physical inventory of envelopes at Harco. Once these figures were acquired, I had a base with which to determine the stock on hand.

4. *Accumulate three-year purchase history of envelopes.* Thirty-five work-sheets on the envelopes were prepared, with separate statistics on price, usage, overshipments, stock, and a general purchase history for each product. It was a huge clerical task that had to be prepared using documents from a manual system. Its value, however, was tremendous in terms of its use in a COM program for envelope purchases.

5. *Ask the vendor for a complete list of stock on hand.* Over the years the vendor had not given an adequate account of the envelopes it held in stock for Harco. I asked for a complete stock list—and got it.

Once this information was accumulated—complete stock list, the purchase history, current counts, and so forth—I could determine the operational and financial status of the envelope products purchased. This brought me back to the 35.4% cash loss on total purchases over the past three years, including the cash giveaway of $42,000.

All the questions had been answered. We now knew why Harco had paid for envelopes it never received: no employee in the company took responsibility for control. Purchasing did not have enough clout for a company of that size and growth. But management did not recognize this, and no other department in the company had come to Purchasing's rescue. Company money was lost or squandered. *It fell below the cash management level-line.* Physical dollars had escaped. This time, however, the cash losses came off the vendor's inventory shelves.

The Clean-Up Campaign

The first thing to do in a clean-up campaign is *stop the losses*. The fact that 35.4% of the envelope purchases were wasted left plenty of room for improvement. At times I don't understand how business people can allow routine business operations to get so far out of hand. But to let you know it *does* happen in business is my object. Such situations will arise in companies, perhaps, in your case, with less impact in procedure control. But then, the dollars could be larger, proportionately. Losses will occur. Let us analyze the problem at Harco by way of illustrating the steps taken to improve cash operations systems and procedures within the company.

What was the biggest cause of profit loss? It was not the vendor, I think we can agree, but the vendor's salesperson. An interesting note here is that, just four months before my review, the Afway Envelope Company salesperson retired from the company, leaving the mess behind.

With that salesperson out of the way, our first task was to salvage the vendor. My client did not relish keeping Afway as the company's envelope vendor, but Harco offered Afway a chance to bid for the account, anyway. Afway had been a quality vendor and their management people were among the best in their approach to business. They could not have been more sympathetic to Harco's problem—except when it came to the dollars involved, specifically, a cash loss of $42,000 over three years.

That was the next subject to discuss with Afway: restitution. Harco wanted serious consideration of its three-year $42,000 profit loss (cash recovery). The company understood that the problem was not totally the fault of the vendor, so Harco wanted to accept $20,000 of the burden on the basis of bad purchase control. Afway Envelope, however, was approached for restitution of $22,000, based on overcharges, overshipments, and the cost of money.

"We couldn't possibly recover that much money in our sales to your client," the Afway vice-president concluded. "It would take years to make it back."

The future was to prove this vice-president wrong, but that was Afway's final decision. They didn't know that the Harco account was about to undergo a growth of 163 percent in envelope purchases in the coming year. Afway's was a short-sighted decision. Over the next five years, Afway could have grossed $500,000 in extra sales volume.

Under normal conditions, we would accept the vice-president's statement as being within reason. After all, it took Afway three years to accumulate the $42,000—at his customer's expense!

We could not salvage the vendor. Afway could not compete with other companies in bidding on the basis of Harco's new envelope price schedule. We did, however, recover $4,434, plus a bonus in artwork dies, before closing the account.

Artwork Inventory

I stumbled onto another valuable cash recovery area—artwork, a much-ignored, high-investment area. Through persistence, I intercepted at least $10,000 worth of artwork from Afway.

Afway had been manufacturing envelopes for my client for years, and was reluctant to give up the artwork for the envelopes. Afway was supposed to return it to the customer after each purchase, however. But that did not happen. In the role of the consultant, I stayed on top of the matter by recovering at least 80 percent of the artwork on trips to Afway's offices while attempting to mend the differences between the companies.

The point here is that artwork, dies, and tooling are an expensive investment for companies. Every effort should be made to control this material through inventory records. For tax purposes, depreciation write-off must also be considered, if these items are capitalized.

Money picked up from cash recovery was returned to my client, for several reasons. The biggest reason was prices, but overpayments for freight and artwork were also returned. We even managed some return of cash because of overshipments. We returned the overshipped quantities above the 10-percent minimum.

Recovering cash for an envelope product is no easy task. It is difficult to identify cash cut-offs in the manufacturing and pricing structure of a printed product. Most envelope companies identify their production process as "job shop," meaning that each order is based on a separate cost structure.

This production process entails paste-up of various artwork dies on a screen (roughly 3 by 3 feet) in which one pass is made over the printing presses for each color. The problem is to run the screen economically. The printer must stay as close as possible to the quantity specified for each envelope product on the screen. If the printer does not stay within quantity limits, considerable waste occurs on low-quantity items on a high-quantity run.

Cash recovery is made difficult because the same envelope, theoretically, could have different prices because of the economics involved in running the presses. I found this to be a problem in analyzing envelope prices for cash recovery. The vendor always had an out: referring back to job costs.

This situation changed, however, when we submitted the new COM program price schedule for outside bids. The successful bid on the new program used the purchase-quantity scale instead of the screen job cost.

We will return to this subject, but, in my opinion, the cash operations approach to screen-process costing is the road to success in the printed-envelope business. What I want to emphasize here, though, is that new profits can be made by evaluating the purchase-price structure on multiline or high-quantity purchase items, regardless of the product involved.

Systems and Procedures Clean-Up Campaign

Now let us look at some methods for improving the systems and procedures used for this multiline product. The purchasing of envelopes of different sizes, colors, and quantity is a difficult challenge for the business executive. In the next few pages we'll see just how big the challenge can be.

Turning the envelope stop-losses problem around was not done overnight. But putting a profit person in charge of the project was a step forward. My interest as a consultant here helped ensure new profits for my client. The job, however, was enormous.

In the envelope stockroom, a number of things were out of line, which prevented profitable procedures from taking hold. The four main ones were:

1. Excessive open space on the shelves. The company was not making good use of its storage facilities.
2. No part number control on the shelves.
3. Envelopes were stored in various rooms throughout the plant. This weakened stockroom production efficiency.
4. Obsolete envelopes, some up to six years old, were stored in prime shelf space.

Improved Utilization of Shelf Space

The first stockroom improvement was to open the lower, more accessible shelves for the high-usage envelopes. The slow movers, which had not been used during the past year, were transferred to a nearby warehouse where they could easily be controlled by a perpetual-inventory system.

Product labels—a paper sticker stored on pasteboard rolls—were also stealing valuable shelf space from high-usage envelopes. These labels controlled five 16-square-foot cubicles, but they were stacked only one foot high in each cubicle. This, of course, wasted three square feet of space in each of the five cubicles. My recommendation was to place the labels on stock racks—hooks resembling broom handles attached horizontally to vertical bars. It worked beautifully. The five cubicles were reduced to one and a half. The space in the other three and a half cubicles opened up valuable storage area for envelopes.

Now the hithertc wasted envelope storage space took on a new image. Shelves were turned over to the numerous fast-moving, high-usage envelopes. Other improvements were also made. Sweepers and dusters were used to clean the area, and aisles were laid out that provided better access to the shelves. New light fixtures were installed, making envelope identification easier. Once the envelope inventory and the usage history were complete, we were ready to stock the shelves.

The Part Number System

Another important change had to be made: shelf identification by part number. Each envelope purchased had a special part number preceded by an alphabetical prefix. Prefix letters went from A to Z, and so did the new stockroom storage system. Another feature was that a single letter would represent a customer's name. When the customer's order came through for a particular envelope, all the envelopes of that size could be located in one place.

The time had come to stock the shelves. In the future the total 16 square feet of space on the shelves would be utilized economically. Boxes of envelopes were brought in and stored in space allocated for 4 turnovers per year or the most economical purchase rate for utilizing the space. Individual envelope controls and quantities fell in like clockwork.

When we brought the production employees into the renovated stockroom on the final day to explain the revised procedures and system, to my surprise they actually applauded the new improvements. It had taken extra effort for them to work in an unorganized supply area. Production employees appreciate the application of new profit ideas in their company.

Benefits

1. The new stockroom provided immediate physical control for production and purchasing employees. Money was saved on future physical inventories, particularly on outside accountant costs.
2. Stock-outs were less likely because now employees could help detect low inventory. This, in turn, made possible fast forwarding of orders to Purchasing in case of a run on a particular item.
3. An "instant locater" was installed for production employees—part numbers were marked on the shelves. It was no longer necessary to use a ladder to find envelopes, resulting in a profit savings in employee-time control.

4. A good morale booster. When management improves working areas in production, employees are more likely to realize that management has their interests in mind, too.

Purchasing Systems Clean-Up

I explained to the company president that there was no basic plan of inventory control for the 80 different envelopes used. There were obsolete orders—in full—on the shelves that were never used or needed. During this period prices were increased progressively and unfairly and without getting competitive bids.

The president's response to this assessment was to ask me to stay on and clean up the mess. The assignment sounded challenging to me, and I went to work.

The purchasing problem had been caused by a lack of product-by-product control. There were 80 different envelopes, which meant that over the course of a year, 3,500 combination decisions had to be made. The purchasing agent should have understood that analysis would be required for each envelope. The PA completely ignored responsibility, which left the door open for the salesperson.

Let us look back at a letter concerning this account. The letter read, in part: "As per our phone conversation, I am entering the following blanket orders for stock in our warehouse. I will advise you of shipment dates as soon as possible."

What did the purchasing agent do? The PA did not question the salesperson or look into whether the purchase was necessary. The salesperson was allowed to make the decision on the purchase order. Actually, it was more what the purchasing agent *did not do*. Following are some errors made by the PA.

1. By letter, the purchasing agent placed an unnecessary purchase order. We had determined that the purchase order had out right purchase losses of 42 percent on the total order. Eight of the 14 envelopes ordered were held by the vendor for more than two years. Price increases were excessively high, and overshipments were atrocious. Probably only 2 of the 14 items were needed.
2. The order was placed by phone. No purchase analysis work was done; nor was any paperwork or purchase orders submitted initially to put the order in progress. The PO was sent later.
3. Blanket orders were issued for warehoused stock. Salespeople had carte blanche to order and place stock on the shelves at the envelope company, although the stock might never be shipped. Nevertheless, my client was expected to pay for the stock, shipped

or not, within 12 months. The salesperson gets a commission, the vendor makes a profit, and my client, because of an incompetent purchasing agent, takes it on the nose.

4. The salesperson made no commitment in writing to indicate that my client was out of stock and that certain quantities must be ordered. No correspondence or paperwork, in either direction, indicated that a usage analysis had been conducted by the salesperson or by my client's purchasing, production, or marketing departments. More than $100,000 in purchases was made by my client's purchasing agent on blind chance alone.

It was clear that the responsibility for the big job in envelope purchases had been ignored. My objective as a consultant would be to pull things together in Purchasing. The salesperson had been given plenty of leeway, which had been used to vendor's advantage. My job now was to reverse this trend.

Our goal was to acquire specific historical statistics with which to determine future usage figures on a multiline product. We would then use the information to establish a base for our envelope purchase control guide. This guide would be the company's ultimate source for future envelope purchases.

Envelope Purchase Control Guide

The envelope purchase control guide was developed to bring together the many parts of a purchase for one envelope product. It is designed to identify usage and control inventory quantities. This should lead eventually to economical benefits in the purchase of envelopes. This guide is a counterpart to the grinding-wheels purchase control manual described in Chapter 6. Both are designed to supply statistical information that, in turn, can provide economically feasible procedures to assist in the procurement of multiline products.

The search for envelope statistics was done manually. I asked for computer support, but that was impossible. Electronic data processing was 20 programs behind at that time; the EDP people could not see their way clear to give a profit program priority over the nonprofit programs. This may sould odd to some business people, but such conduct is common in the major proportion of American corporations. COM programs are designed in part to change this attitude. For COM purposes, though, outside computer services are recommended, and they can easily be paid for.

Thus our envelope statistical program was done manually. The search was conducted by one person, supported by employees and took 60 research hours. Here is an account of the work completed in the usage and inventory areas.

Usage History

My first step in preparing the envelope purchase guide was to develop a purchase history for each envelope purchased during the past three years (the product-by-product usage approach). Those purchases, barring obsolete throwaways, were added to quantities in current inventories. This total, divided by the number of months that had expired, would be the average monthly usage.

The average monthly usage was then divided into current inventory balances, which would equal the average number of months of stock in my client's inventory. This is simple arithmetic, but to record the process when 80 different items are involved becomes a huge task for company employees. The cash losses that resulted because this simple arithmetic wasn't performed, however, were extremely high.

There were other factors to be considered. We had to keep close watch on the in-plant inventory. In any three-month period there could be a run on a particulr envelope, which might distort the usage rate. Also, if obsolete orders were thrown away instead of being sent to my client's plant with no traceable receipts, our figures could be misconstrued. We were lucky; no unforeseen problems occurred, and our statistics remained constant.

A three-year usage history is a useful base as long as production remains at a measurable level. (This also depends on the product; a three-year history can be wasted on a product with a high turnover rate.) A three-year history on envelopes, however, because of low annual turnover, is an excellent base as long as purchases and current inventory status can be depended on. If they are dependable, then usage figures should be as solid as rock.

When I was satisfied that the usage histories were ready, I could forecast future purchase quantities.

Inventory Statistics

We used current, accurate, physical inventories. When I divided the most up-to-date usages into these inventories, I could determine what quantity of envelopes would have to be purchased, in what quantities for a price break, right down to the date on which they would be purchased.

The surprising part of this was the accuracy of the envelope purchase guide. I forecasted purchases as far as three years in the future. When I checked back with the manager of envelope control a couple of years later, he reported that the forecast had been remarkably accurate. The secret is to go back to the base. The longer your purchase history, the stronger your usage base. This applies to all purchased and manufactured products when a measurable production and inventory-turnover process is in operation.

The above purchase information served ultimately as the answer for envelope inventory control at Harco. This usage and purchase forecast was originally entered on 36-column worksheets. In time, the complete control system was transferred to large control cards the size and stock of a standard manila folder (see Figure 10.1).

The control card keeps a perpetual record of purchases, as well as a history of purchases, on the front and the back. It also registers the annual usage and quantity breakpoint for price. Two other very important points are freight (Was it included in the price?), and purchase price (Was it based on a contract price or a regular price?). The card or the control worksheet is an easy update record and in terms of cash operations management it is a key to multiple profit dollars for companies. Do not interpret this card as a perpetual inventory control—it is a purchase control card.

Envelope Price Schedule

I stated in my consultant's report to the company president "that the envelope price schedule is a vital tool for multiquantity envelope-buying. It will provide an accurate price guide for each size and specification (style, quantities, color, paper, etc.) of envelope purchased. It establishes an open price base for the seller as well as the buyer." Once the benefits of the schedule were explained, the president was eager to put it to use."

When I got into the envelope-pricing area, several things were happening to my client's envelope prices. Here are a few:

1. Large orders (30,000 envelopes) were costing less in total amount than smaller orders (10,000) for the same envelope.
2. There were increases in quantities of orders but no corresponding decreases in price.
3. Small envelopes sometimes carried higher prices than large envelopes, with the same quantity ordered.
4. From one order to the next, there were price increases that ranged as high as 200 percent on the same envelopes.
5. Prices for the same envelope in different sizes were not synchronized. Small envelopes cost as much as large ones, which violated every principle of quantity-price-break buying.
6. Price increases were far out of synchronization. Large quantities of orders were increased by 50 to 200 percent over the three previous

Figure 10.1 Usage and purchase forecast control card

DESCRIPTION ______________________ Deliver to Dept. No. ______________

Purchase Negotiated – Contract/Regular

1		2		3	
Manufacturer		Manufacturer		Manufacturer	
Vendor Desc.		Vendor Desc.		Vendor Desc.	
Supplier		Supplier		Supplier	
Qty		Qty		Qty	
Price		Price		Price	
Price		Price		Price	
Price		Price		Price	

P.O. No.	Vendor No.	Ordered Date	Ordered Quantity	P.O. Unit Cost	Received Date	Received Quantity	Balance	P.O. No.	Vendor No.	Ordered Date	Ordered Quantity	P.O. Unit Cost	Received Date	Received Quantity	Balance

Comments:

Freight Included			Annual Average Usage	Quantity Break Point
Vend	Yes	No		
1				
2				
3				

years. More than 58 percent of the orders were increased 20 to 50 percent. These increases occurred when a 2- to 3-percent price-increase economy was in effect. The table below is an analysis of price increases during that three-year period:

Percent dollar purchases	Percent price increase	
12.6	9 to 20	
58.2	20 to 50	
10.1	50 to 75	equals 29.1
13.9	75 to 100	percent of
5.1	100 to 200	dollars purchased
100		

This pricing structure was clearly in need of realignment. As mentioned earlier concerning the screen process, the job-cost system of manufacturing envelopes did not have a consistent price structure. Thus, here, we needed a new idea in pricing if we were to organize and synchronize the cost of envelopes. Once the percentages (given in the table above) were established, the only alternative was to get the pricing aligned or move away from it and let it die. I could not accept the idea that this was the only way to price envelopes; so I took on the envelope pricing challenge.

The Purchase Price Theory

I went to work on envelope prices with a new theory in mind: include the vendor in the program as much as possible. This approach may seem contrary to business practice, but it looked like the best approach to purchasing multiline products.

My theory was to give the vendor all information that could be accumulated on my client's envelopes—except past prices. This included the information on the 80 different envelopes purchased by my client. The vendor would receive complete usage rates as well as all specifications (style, quantity, weight, and so on). The vendor was even issued a copy of the three-year forecast of the dates on which my client expected to buy.

Why give the vendor so much information? There were several reasons. Annual purchases of 80 different envelopes is a tremendous volume for a supplier, particularly when the customer is expecting a future, long-term annual volume of $200,000. More important, this quantitive information was passed on so the vendor could prepare quotes for a long-term package-purchase deal. Let's look into the background of the other reasons:

1. This much information had never been given to the vendor before; the vendor had been kept in the dark. It was impossible to plan economical moves for my client because the vendor was not aware of the customer's needs. For that matter, the customer—my client—did not know his own needs. Harco was in no position to issue long-term information to its vendors. Harco had not used a purchase control manual in its purchase activities.

2. If the vendor were given total usage and volume information, the vendor could work it into the vendor's overall production cycle. Envelope companies must make commitments to their paper suppliers. The more information they have about their customers' needs, the better prices they can negotiate from their suppliers. These prices, of course, are passed along to customers in a competitive situation.

3. The vendor will go all-out to get the customer's business. The vendor can see the benefits in issuing a low price for high volume. The winning part of this business relationship is that both parties make commitments. Once the quotes are in, the customer can weigh the facts and choose a vendor.

The most important aspect of the disclosure procedure is finding out what vendor's capabilities are. It requires the vendor to expose weaknesses as well as strong points, which can benefit the vendor as well if a long-term commitment is made to the customer.

How Does the Vendor Make Commitments?

The vendor makes commitments through the envelope price schedule. Actually this schedule should be identified as an organized, competitive bid. With any product other than envelopes, boxes, or the like, this would be considered a normal approach to a purchase. But printed envelopes are different.

This gets us back to the subject of making economical runs across the printing press screen. It also has to do with the customer's knowledge of usage. If the customer can pinpoint the date of future purchases, using the purchase control manual, align this with the vendor's purchase commitments for paper, and identify specific jobs that fit the vendor's production screen format—then a triangle is formed. An envelope price schedule can be issued by the vendor for a price quote on a graduated-quantity, color (flexograph or lithograph), or size basis.

The key to the matter is for both the vendor and the user to know the total estimated usage, which means coordinating vendor purchase-of-paper commitments with production scheduling of the number of jobs issued by the user.

Again, we note that there were 80 active envelopes in Harco's product line. The success of the price schedule given above depends on giving a responsible vendor a six-month, qualified commitment to purchase certain amounts on certain dates. Once the amounts are determined, quotes should be given to the best envelope producers that can be found. A facsimile of the envelope price schedule is given in Figure 10.2. This brings us back to John Farnsworth. The interesting part about this pricing structure is that only a couple of companies, out of eight, could complete the schedule satisfactorily. The other companies couldn't stay within the guidelines or quantities, or if they stayed within the quantity/price allotment area, their prices were not in line with Farnsworth's prices.

Interestingly, one of the five companies had exceptionally good prices on the small-to-medium-quantity envelope orders but could not compete on a large-quantity orders. (The company must have had a secret in producing lower quantities.) This helped round out our program.

The good news about the schedule was that both companies had maintained their hold on the Harco account over the years. Also, since the advent of the price schedule, Harco had had a couple of other companies that made successful bids for some of the business. Most important, the current envelope prices were made retroactive to the level of three years previous. The importance of good inventory control and an organized price schedule has greatly improved cash profits for Harco.

Artwork Inventory

Envelope artwork costs can be expensive. Usually, because artwork, dies, and tools are reusable, in time the investment can be depreciated, as can any normal asset.

With this in mind, it pays to establish an artwork inventory in your company. Harco had no such inventory, yet the company had always paid cash for artwork on each envelope purchased. The interesting part about this situation is that no one at Harco took much interest in the artwork. The fact that Harco was about to change envelope vendors and was about to pay for new artwork impressed no one.

I quickly moved into this area. At the same time, I asked Bill Busky for help, which I got. Bill understood every aspect of the new purchase control manual and the envelope price schedule. He agreed to dig into the artwork inventory. Together, he and I established a $10,000 artwork file on the old artwork, which Harco was mistakenly planning to leave with the old vendor.

Bill looked around and came up with an engineering file cabinet for storing the artwork. Eventually we pulled practically all the artwork in and gradually built up the file from new vendor purchases. Today, the

Figure 10.2. Envelope Price Schedule.

Size	Description	Estimated 6-Month Usage	Quantity		Flexographic One-color		Lithographic Two-color
1-⅞ x 3-⅞	Open End	615M	10M	....	23.00	....	56.00
	Extended latex		15M	....	19.00	....	38.00
	flap		25M	....	14.50	....	25.00
	32# White Kraft		50M	....	10.50	....	16.50
			100M	....	8.90	....	12.00
2-½ x 4-¼	Open End	215M	10M	....	21.00	....	53.00
	Extended latex		15M	....	17.00	....	34.00
	flap		25M	....	12.00	....	24.50
	32# White Kraft		50M	....	9.00	....	16.00
			100M	....	8.00	....	12.00
			250M	....	7.00	....	11.00
2-⅝ x 3-¼	Open End	75M	10M	....	24.00	....	55.00
	Extended latex		15M	....	19.00	....	38.00
	flap		25M	....	14.00	....	25.00
	32# White Kraft		50M	....	10.50	....	17.00
			100M	....	9.00	....	12.00
3 x 5	Open End	250M	10M	....	36.00	....	56.00
	Extended latex		15M	....	29.00	....	48.00
	flap		25M	....	23.00	....	35.00
	110# White Index		50M	....	18.00	....	24.00
			100M	....	16.00	....	18.00
3 x 5	Open End	250M	10M	....	33.00	....	60.00
	Extended latex		15M	....	25.00	....	49.00
	flap		25M	....	19.00	....	33.00
	7 Pt. Manila		50M	....	14.00	....	20.00
			100M	....	12.00	....	17.50
4 x 5	Open End	100M	10M	....	39.00	....	59.00
	Extended latex		15M	....	31.00	....	50.00
	flap		25M	....	25.00	....	38.00
	110# White Index		50M	....	20.00	....	25.00
			100M	....	17.00	....	21.00
3-½ x 6-¾	Open End	150M	10M	....	43.00	....	64.00
	Extended latex		15M	....	33.00	....	52.00
	flap		25M	....	26.00	....	38.00
	110# White Index		50M	....	22.00	....	31.00
			100M	....	19.00	....	23.00

artwork file is valued at about $20,000. It bears repeating that this new-found asset was the result of an idea that originated in cash operations management.

Technical Ideas for Lower Prices

How would you like to achieve a 50-percent reduction in price on 60 percent of a product line you purchased for your company? Any business executive would jump at the chance, I'm sure.

A value-analysis attempt to do this was successful at Harco. The technical improvement in the product that resulted made a big difference in COM profit dollars.

My value-analysis review of the envelopes showed that the 2-by-3-inch envelopes were made from the same 125-pound stock as the 4-by-6-inch envelopes. The smaller envelope weighed much less. Why, then, did it require such heavy stock? The fact is, it did not require heavy stock. We were able to reduce the 2-by-3 envelopes from 125-pound stock to 32-pound. The 3-by-4 envelopes were reduced to 110 stock; the 5-by-6 inch envelopes remained at the same weight.

The benefit in economy in this case was that the 2 x 3 envelopes represented 60 percent of the total purchase volume. This was the source of the savings. Sixty percent of $100,000 volume, reduced by a 50-percent price reduction, amounted to a future annual cash operations management profit of $30,000.

One drawback must be mentioned. After a couple of years some customers complained of breakage of the 32-pound paper. Depending on how serious this is in customer service, consideration must be given to upgrading stock. Such upgrading should be a well-thought-out decision on the part of management, who should carefully consider the values involved. It is important that management not make hasty decisions to return to the original stock.

Envelopes COM Program Benefits

cash recovery	Amount
price deficiencies	
overshipment returns	$ 4,434
Freight overpayments	
Artwork inventory (from prior vendor)	$10,000
total cash recovery	$14,434
Systems and Procedures	
stockroom improvements (estimated labor-saving ideas)	6,000
purchase control guide (future inventory control)	$12,000
envelope price schedule (future price control)	$10,000
artwork inventory	$ 5,000
technical improvements	$20,000
total annual savings	$53,000
total first-year benefits	$67,434

What Are the Advantages of a Control Manual?

Now that we've seen applications of the price manual and the inventory control manual, the question might be asked, What are their advantages? The question is best answered with another, What would be your reaction if your vendor announced a price increase of 9 percent to become effective within the next 30 days?

Your first thought would probably be to wonder whether you need the product within the next 30 or even 60 days. Here is where the multiline purchase control manual can give you an immediate answer.

Once you determine that you need the product, and in what quantity, you can determine the cash outlay by using your product price schedule. Then you compare the savings from early purchase with the cost of shelving. Chances are, you will uncover a profit—and probably a considerable one—in 100-percent cash dollars.

Let's face it: you are going to buy and pay for this product in two to four weeks, regardless. Why not use your control manuals to order now, for a 9 percent savings? You will have the necessary information in the manual for ready reference and immediate savings.

It is surprising how few companies take advantage of such a money-making approach to purchasing. In today's inflationary economy it can pay big dividends to study your needs and purchase ahead of price increases. This would be a specific company assignment for a "profit person."

The Profit Picture

Annual gross profits at Harco were approximately $400,000 on a sales volume of nearly $12 million, or 3.3%. When we compare these figures with the anticipated annual benefits of our envelope COM program ($53,000; see Figure 10.3), we are talking about an estimated 13 percent addition to profits, plus $14,434 in cash recovery. This is a remarkable benefit in any business, especially for the purchase of one multiline product.

The overall format of cash operations management was firmly established at Harco. The type of deficiencies analyzed there were spread throughout the company. There were reasons for Harco's poor profit picture; the COM review had revealed them. From this point on, profits were in the hands of the company president and his team. I had shown them that more profits were waiting to be made through an extended COM program.

Figure 10.3 Total envelope COM program

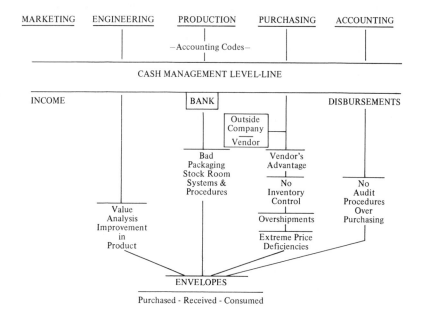

Summary

Vendor's advantage proved a culprit again. When the purchasing department has no defense against profit loss, the vendor has carte blanche to take profits from its customer. This happened in the Harco envelope-purchase case.

Products were purchased through inadequate systems and procedures. The vendor's salesperson recognized these weaknesses and took advantage of them. I recognized the vendor's advantage when applying COM principles in my client's profit-improvement program. The client stopped the cash losses by improving the company's systems and procedures of cash management through purchasing.

Improvements were made, first by stabilizing physical control, by new stockroom procedures, and by new systems applications. This involved labor-saving ideas and improved storage facilities. Second, a product control guide was developed to ensure proper inventory control. The third improvement was the introduction of an envelope price schedule, which reversed prices back to a level of three years prior. This was a planned price guide used to develop good purchase techniques, a concept applicable to numerous products. Other additions to the envelope-purchase system were the artwork inventory file and value-analysis profit improvement by introducing new technical ideas concerning the product.

The complete improved envelope program summarized here is successful because of the use of cash operations management procedures to control a business's purchasing and inventory. Improvements came not only through cash recovery but through improvements in systems and procedures. All new profits were derived below the cash management level-line.

Questions on Chapter 10

PURCHASING AND INVENTORY CONTROL

1. What assurances does your company president have that purchase and inventory control systems and procedures are adequate?
2. Are your purchasing managers and clerical people practicing good business-control principles in purchase and inventory systems and procedures?
3. Do your purchasing people do analyses of usage and inventory balances before purchases are made?
4. How extensive are the analysis procedures for your company's miltiline products?
5. Is your purchasing agent overloaded with purchase responsibilities?

6. Does your purchasing agent have a chance to learn the usage rate of all products purchased?

7. What procedures does your purchasing agent follow in determining usage?

8. Has a system been developed for your multiline products to assist the purchasing agent in identifying usage, for example, the envelope purchase control guide?

9. How difficult is it for your purchasing agent to determine quantities of future purchases? Does the PA have a reference control that can give usage statistics quickly?

10. Does your company have a computer record of usage analysis? Has a systems audit been conducted on this EDP program recently?

11. How accurate are the purchase statistics that go into your computer purchase-usage program? Have you checked them recently?

12. Would a manual usage-control system improve your EDP usage-control system? (A cash operations management program will answer this question.)

13. Does your company use a product-by-product approach to determine usage of all its purchased and manufactured parts?

14. Have you noticed extraordinary obsolescence in your inventories?

15. Does your company keep an inventory of the purchased products at your vendor's warehouse?

16. What controls are placed on outside-warehouse inventories?

17. Are your purchasing people cooperating with the inventory control people in your company?

18. Are your inventory control people supplying inventory figures to Purchasing, as well as to other management people?

19. How often is your inventory analyzed for excessively high product balances? What steps are taken when such is discovered?

20. Who is in charge at your company of making sure that every possible tool is employed to assist purchasing and inventory control people in applying the most profitable techniques in their work?

21. What purchase history is kept for each product in inventory? Do the balances in your inventory coincide with monthly usage rates?

22. What form is used to record a product-purchase history—a loose-leaf control form, a purchase history card, index card?

23. What information is kept in the history record? Are usage, quantity break, current inventory balance, price, freight disposition, and PO numbers kept?

24. What price control governs your multiline products? Contracts? Special price lists? Price control guides?

25. What concept or concepts of purchase theory are behind your multiline products? Would it help to involve your vendor more deeply in your general planning?
26. Does your company offer complete usage and purchase-volume information to your vendors? Are your company systems capable of supplying this information?

ARTWORK, DIES, AND TOOLING

27. Does your company own artwork, dies, and tools that are currently in the possession of your vendors?
28. Do you keep an inventory record of your artwork, dies, and tools?
29. Do your accountants know that you own artwork? Are they taking into account the depreciation on this asset?

TECHNICAL IMPROVEMENTS

30. Has a value analysis been conducted on your multiline purchased products recently?
31. What benefits might your company derive from value analysis improvements on your purchased products?

11. A Multimillion Dollar Systems Error: Marketing, Billing, Distribution, and Cash

The Widget Manufacturing Company of America, Inc., is a large company with a massive manufacturing plant six stories high and two city blocks long, located in the heart of a small town in the Midwest. The town provides about 2,500 workers for the company. Their loyalty to the company is beyond reproach. Some have worked for the Widget Company for 50 years. They are devoted to their families and to the company. This devotion, combined with their skill in using their hands, has made the company the best producers of widgets in the United States.

Since early in this century, Widget has with pride and satisfaction provided products to its customers. When someone shopped for a dependable widget, this brand was usually selected.

Then one day a conglomerate bought up the Widget company, and in time less interest and attention were shown to the widget-makers. Next came a flow of mediocre managers. It wasn't long before the dependable reputation of the company had slipped. Customers complained about both the product and the service; the managers at corporate headquarters complained about profits.

It was at this point that I introduced my COM program. Introductions were made, and the histories of profits and loss were laid before me. My goal was to determine the cause of profit decline and find the reason why customers were complaining about the product.

The COM Marketing Review

I began with a two-foot stack of customer invoices that had just come from the computer. The job, I figured, would take a three-week preliminary review, plus another three weeks to implement improvements in the company's systems and procedures. By reviewing the customer invoices, I would familiarize myself with the products and learn the intricacies of Widget's billing system. In due time I would interview employees and develop an overall picture of departmental responsibilities and activities. The departments highlighted in my review, initially, would be Marketing, Billing, and Production and their supporting subdepartments. What I had not realized was how broad the program would become. Soon I was to find out.

A Widget Company salesperson hastened through the swinging doors of the Retsky Building in downtown Detroit one afternoon in September. This was the corporate home office of the Retsky Department Store chain, a well-known merchandiser in the Midwest. He waited for an elevator. When the doors of one opened, the salesperson stepped in quickly, then pushed the button for 7. The seventh floor was Retsky's reception floor, as well as where the purchasing department was located. His name was Wesley Warber and he had been summoned upstairs by a customer.

"Yes, Mr. Warber," the receptionist said after he got out at the seventh floor. "Mr. Benson has been expecting you. Please go in."

"That usually means trouble," Wesley reminded himself as he opened the door to Benson's office. Some people were already gathered there, huddling over what appeared to be a stack of Widget invoices.

"Wesley," Benson called from across the room, "we were just discussing your widget invoices. Come in—we have a problem."

Benson talked fast, wasting no words. Wesley placed his attaché case on a chair and joined the group.

"Here, Wesley; look at these invoices. There are thirty-six of them. You see these invoices? Would you believe that they all belong to the same purchase order, and that the order still is not complete? What are you guys doing to us over there? We can't cope with a back-order situation like this. Here, our processing costs are thirty-six times what they should be on the business we do with Widgets. Your billing costs must be outrageous."

Warber could find nothing to say. This was his first run-through on the back-order problem. What could he say? Benson was right.

"Something else, Wesley," Benson continued, "this order was originated in March. It was set up for our "Graduation promotion in early June. We had all our advertising in the papers, and your people couldn't deliver our products. Here you are six months later, still shipping to us in drips and drabs. We lost money on this, and on others like it in the past, but we don't intend to lose again. Go back to your people and tell them to shape up or we'll take our business to another widget line.

Another salesperson from the Widget Manufacturing Company was summoned to Kansas City, where he was told: "We have just received forty-seven cartons of widgets with price stickers from Kober Brothers Stores in Los Angeles on them, marked at $2.78 each. First, we don't appreciate getting Kober's reject widgets and second, we don't understand how Kober can sell these widgets for $2.78 each, when they cost us $2.77 as distributors."

A Phoenix retailer said: "We don't understand why orders written in October don't arrive until January. Give us receivables dating we'll use them for Mother's Day, graduation, and Father's Day. Otherwise, we return them."

A Boston wholesaler located in a large office building on Washington Street complained: "The widgets we ordered for our graduation promotion didn't arrive until *September*. That was advertising dollars we put into local promotions—and so did you, since we go halves on promotions."

By now you may be wondering what the point of these sales stories is. The stories, I believe, make their point in the customer-service situation at the Widget Manufacturing Company of America. I have included these anecdotes to clarify the customer-service problem.

Consultants generally keep their work to themselves. By tradition, they are usually bound to silence. But findings in their work also bind them to confidentiality. Once a woman in an office asked me how I could keep the huge dollar-profit savings for my clients so quiet and tied up inside. "I should think you would be shouting it from the rooftops," she said.

When it is my life's work, however, I cannot afford such antics. Just such a situation was building up for me at the corporate headquarters of Widget. The potential for big profit savings was becoming obvious.

My work was completed on the stack of Widget invoices. From this introduction, I noticed a couple of odd things. One was the invoice amounts of $2 to $8, which were numerous. How could a company process an order, pick and ship it, through the factory, and run a computer invoice for less than $8, not to mention the two-dollar invoice? Another question concerned the large quantity of invoices sent to the customer as back orders. The numbers and percentages seemed dangerously high.

Once the two-dollar invoices surfaced, I conducted a special review of 1,800 shipments sent to a five-and-dime store's customer. Approximately 700 of the shipments (38.8%) proessed were in amounts less than $8 each. When you take into account the cost of the product, and the freight and incremental costs of processing the shipment, all of these orders had to have been processed at a loss.

Customer Service Interviews

My interviews got underway after the invoice survey. In time I would talk to all the managers of customer service, advertising, national sales, special products, and sales administration, including the marketing vice-president. Initially, however, I settled for the customer service manager, Steve Merrill.

Usually opening interviews are somewhat subdued, but not with this man. He didn't hold back a thing when I explained the purpose of the interview. "Yes, I think we have profit problems in marketing. But our problems start further down the line. We see things happening that should be taken care of by other managers."

"Let's take it step by step," I said. What about the small invoices? What part do they play in the problem?"

"They are a by-product of a back-order problem," Merrill replied. "The reason they fall out is that we ship direct to retail outlets of the big chain discount stores. It's a new policy, just to get sales out the door. Back orders came out in very small denominations. Products were not in inventory when the computer indicated shipment."

This was getting into technical areas, so I changed the topic for the moment. "Steve, what about those back orders? How big of a problem are they?"

"Back orders! They *are* the problem."

My interviews with the other middle-level managers revealed the same problem: back orders. The trouble with a subject as broad as back orders is the number of causes, as well as the costly profit problems they lead to. This was a problem for the cash operations management program. We were ready to zero in on the back-order systems problem at Widget.

COM in Marketing

What is a back order? A customer back order is an additional billing on an incomplete purchase order, on products or items on a purchase order that were not shipped to the customer as part of the original shipment. Back orders originate in various parts of an organization. Back orders are one of the easiest problems for an industry to pick up—and one of the most difficult to cure. Widget Manufacturing was suffering from the problem. My task, as a business consultant, was to solve the problem.

In developing a plan for solving the back-order problem, I took the approach of identifying the negative statistics that surrounded the problem. This involved additional processing costs and led to additional systems problems. If processing a multiline purchase order requires two invoices or three or more (such as 36 invoices at Retsky's), obviously it will cost a company more dollars to process the extra work. This extra work will, in turn, affect numerous employees in various departments, not to mention the extra work for the customer's employees. Let's follow my steps in determining the problems within Widget's marketing structure.

Historical Records Review

The archives at Widget were at the farthest possible point from the main offices. These were the files that contained the company records. To reach the storage area I had to take a five-minute walk into the depths of the plant, board a large freight elevator, and take a slow ride down two floors. Once I was there, the gates of the darkened storage cage were unlocked to allow entry to the files.

In these files were all the sales invoices billed to customers in past years or for the number of years that the IRS required. I was interested only in the past three years. I wanted to determine the number of invoices used each year to bill the company's sales.

The job was easier that I expected. Invoice numbers for the three years in question were in the proper sequence. They could be traced to the day, week, and month. I simply recorded the invoice numbers for 12-month periods, as well as the year-end date, up to the current date.

The invoice numbers revealed some interesting facts. The sales volume over the past three years held steady at $60 million, yet, in the past year, the number of invoices jumped from 48,000 to 63,000—an increase of 15,000, or 31.2%, in invoices issued—a remarkable change for a marketing processing function.

Several things could account for such an increase, among them, back orders. Also, because sales held at the same volume but invoices increased greatly in number, more invoices had to be entered in lower amounts. The two- to eight-dollar invoices would have played an important part in the increase, but other factors were involved. Let's determine how great a price was paid in additional annual processing costs and in profit problems related to back orders and customer service.

A Procedures Review and the Marketing of COM Program Systems

Increased Processing Costs on Back Orders

The sale is made and the raw materials have been purchased. Production must then provide the product. The delivery date is set and the product is shipped. The customer is content and happy. This is the ideal sales pattern for processing an order through a marketing department. But *other* steps are involved in shipping an order, steps that are equally important and that are *costly*.

For example, to ship an order from the Widget Company, the following had to be done: (1) the computer must print a packing slip and invoice to initiate the order; computer time, forms, and handling are cost factors; (2) a shipping clerk must pick the order from inventory; (3) the clerk must package and label the container; (4) the shipping notice and special instructions must be authorized by the billing department; (5) route and carrier instructions must be determined by the traffic department; (6) final handling must be processed by the shipping clerk to the freight truck.

The approximate incremental cost of these steps as well as, perhaps, some others, was approximately $7.76 per single line order. This was the cost figure needed to calculate the dollars of increased process costs on the additional invoices used during the prior year. The process cost was determined by multiplying 15,000 invoices by the cost per invoice (using one item per invoice)—$7.76—which totaled $116,400.

Increased Processing Cost of Freight

When there is an increase in shipments of 15,000 invoices, there are bound to be increased freight costs. In the above case, there were substantial increased freight costs.

A special review I conducted on 116 shipments, using transportation department documents, divulged some information of deep concern to the management people at Widget. I used actual back-order documents on orders ready to be placed on the truck and shipped. This was as deep as I could go in cash operations to get documentation. My statistics revealed that back orders increased freight costs by approximately 40 percent. The Widget Company paid freight on all back orders. It was likely that most of the 15,000 additional orders applied to extra freight costs, and most of these at a minumum charge.

There were two other important reasons for the current year's increased freight costs: bulk shipments through warehouses were cut off at midmonth, which converted bulk freight to a single-shipment price base; and a strong monthly shipping cycle distributed 40 percent of sales from the central distribution center over the last two days of each month. This disrupted the flow of shipments, affected order inquiries, and caused sales cancellations, often after goods had already been shipped. Thus freight was paid both ways.

Freight costs increased over the past year from approximately $1.22 million to $1.64 million (less $122,000 due to rate increases). The balance of $298,000 reflected the freight inefficiencies listed above.

Fewer products were shipped in this particular year than in the previous two years.

Increased Sales Cancellation Costs

Sales cancellations during the current year were $2,455,000, compared to $708,000 during the previous year, an increase of 347 percent, which was surprising for one year. The $708,000 is a dismal cancellation performance, but to lose $2.45 million in sales volume is a blight on sales principles. At the typical widget profit margin of 40 percent (at the cost of manufacturing line), the profit decrease was $698,800.

Back orders, again, were at the heart of the poor customer-service situation. Customers were now enforcing "cancel all back orders" clauses in their orders.

Analysis revealed that no single product continued as a significant cancellation group. This indicated that production satisfied sales orders over a two- to three-month period. We also determined that 64.8 percent of the cancellations were in high-turnover products, which indicated any of several problem functions or a combination of low inventory, poor production output, and an oversell situation (one that was beyond production capacity). In a point-of-purchase-product industry, these are indeed poor customer-service conditions.

Increased Number of Credit Memos

Customer returns written during the past year amounted to $243,000. At a profit margin of 40 percent, the loss of profit was $97,200. The principal causes for the credits were delay in delivery, the use of incorrect modes or routing of shipments, and shipment after cancellation.

Increased Warehousing Costs

Inadequate warehouse cash operations procedures contributed to increased processing costs over the past year. This problem had to do with considerably higher commission rates paid at some distribution warehouses, compared to lower cost bases at other warehouses.

The point here is that the cost structure at the Dallas and Los Angeles warehouses was based on a commission rate, whereas a rental rate was used in Philadelphia and an owner's rate in Atlanta. The commissions were, for example, 1.9¢ per dollar of product shipped from the warehouse, versus .9¢ for the rented space. The total dollar cost increased with increased sales volume shipped from the commission-rate warehouses. This cost, of course, remained constant at the rented and owned warehouses.

To illustrate, during the past year 44 percent of rented-warehouse sales were shipped through Philadelphia, yet this warehouse accounted for only 32 percent of rented-warehouse costs (.9¢ per dollar shipped). The Dallas and Los Angeles warehouses combined had only 12 percent more shipments (56 percent), but because of the commission rate they absorbed 68 percent of the total warehouse costs. The additional warehouse cash dollars cost, in relation to total volume shipments, commission over rental, was $109,440. Benefits could be derived by developing a different approach to warehousing costs.

Widget's COM Program Benefits

Annual systems and procedures losses
Processing costs

Increased shipments caused by back orders; 31.2% increase in the number of invoices processed (48,000 vs. 63,000) caused annual increased incremental costs of (15,000 invoices (times $7.76 estimated cost per invoice)	$ 116,400
Increased cost of freight	
freight costs increase over previous year due to 15,000 additional shipments, returns, cancellations, systems incompetencies	$ 298,000
Increased sales cancellations	
an increase of 347 percent in sales cancellations caused an estimated decrease in profits	$ 698,800
Increased credit memos	
customer returns attributed to poor customer service and back orders amount to $243,000; 40 percent margin, the estimated loss of profits were	$ 97,200
Increased processing costs of warehousing	
Warehousing costs overcharged on commission rate verses rented rate, due to higher volume of shipments	$ 109,440
total marketing processing losses (annual cost prior to COM program)	$1,319,840

What COM marketing benefits did the Widget Company realize from the above analysis? In this instance, only systems and procedural benefits were revealed by the analysis. No particular cash recovery skills were exercised, thus no cash was expected, even though such applications were suitable.

The bulk of the problem here, as we understood from the outset, was in marketing and physical distribution systems and procedures. The initial part of my review consisted of identifying and exposing actual cash dollar losses. This was done by applying COM program skills, which provided an excellent, $1.3 million profit base through processing costs.

As the program was continued, we switched the emphasis to how the business was conducted through departmental operations. We made in-depth systems studies to determine the causes of the poor customer service within the company.

Systems Improvement Review

Customer Service and Physical Distribution

My report to management read:
> A review of back orders indicates a functional problem in the areas of customer service and physical distribution. In addition to increased processing costs we believe there is a 5% to 10% loss of annual sales due to the unsatisfactory level of customer service. This would amount to an estimated $1.8 to $3.5 million loss of annual gross profits.

This came as something of a surprise to Widgets' executive officers. An estimated $2 million annual profit loss was involved. Improvements in the company's systems would practically double current earnings. What could have caused a $2 million to $3 million annual profit loss in a $60-million business?

Identifying the Analysis and Evaluation Areas

What approach should be taken to illustrate to management people that they could increase profits from *within* their own company by 60 to 70 percent annually? The task of explanation and documentation is enormous, but I knew that if the statistics were available, the job could be done.

I started with the company's 3.3% earnings-to-sales ratio. A COM program of this calibre is known to be capable of producing a 3- to 5-percent improvement in the profit-to-sales ratio. A COM program must convincingly establish what can affect broad functional dollar areas in an organization. To implement large dollar changes would require changes in ideas and theories on the part of decision making managers. The dollar values must be impressive. That is exactly what my COM analysis provided for the Widgets Company executives—impressive figures. Here are a few one-liners I used to outline the benefits of the COM program:

Seventy-five percent of back-order items were adequately stocked in the warehouses.

The master production plan decreased inventories 58 percent below the sales forecast on a test of three high-volume product lines.

Shipment cutoffs to the warehouses at midmonth caused 38 percent of the back-ordering.

Forty to fifty percent of back-order dollars were the result of a distribution problem.

Fifty to sixty percent of back-order dollars were the result of a production problem.

New products were not ready when ad promotions were released to the media.

The monthly sales shipment cycle was out of balance for proper product flow.

Forty percent of sales were shipped on the last two days of the month, every month.

There was no item-by-item inventory control on the distribution of more than 1,150 products.

The analysis and evaluation areas of this customer service and distribution problem were, as noted, numerous, the deeper the penetration, the more extensive the problem became. Each area evaluated opened up other reasons why back-order profits fell out of the company's physical distribution system.

Physical distribution is defined as the flow of orders and materials in the business organization. These include (1) sales forecasting, (2) production scheduling, (3) inventory control, (4) warehousing control, (5) order processing, (6) quality control, and (7) advertising and promotion. The implementation of improved systems and procedures in all of the above determines to a large extent the success of customer service on sales.

The solution to the customer-service problem at the Widget Company is represented by all of the above functions. Some of the functions must interact in order to meet the desired customer service levels, particularly sales forecasting, production scheduling, and inventory control. In cash operations management, however, we must look to dollars expended for profits.

Inefficiencies in the Physical Distribution System

Sales Forecasting

For the month of May, the master production plan showed a 58-percent inventory reduction in a test conducted on the three top product lines. This was matched with the same period of the prior year. A second five-month test indicated that production was below the sales forecast by as much as 40 percent.

When testing reveals such negative inventory and production statistics, it must be that sales forecasts were ignored, resulting in the undoing of the good work done by many of the company's employees. Included among these employees are the sales people who made commitments to their customers, as well as the marketing and planning people who set sales quotas and plan promotions. Ignoring sales forecasts disrupts the flow of production, since procurement and production planning, schedule and route sheets, labor tasks, and inventory usage must be changed. The most adverse result of this practice, however, is that it disrupts the delivery of the company's products to customers. In short, it causes a back order.

Why did management cut back on its inventory costs? This is a major part of maintaining prompt delivery of the product. One reason given was pressure to reduce inventories. Thus inventories on the top-line products were reduced because they were the easiest to control, according to the division controller. The other products in the line apparently had little or no inventory control or guidelines.

New Products

The introduction of new products must be done cautiously. Be sure you are aware of both the pitfalls and the potential. The Widgets Company appeared to have been pushing products it could not produce. New products were a big part of this push.

My COM analysis revealed that 94 of 477 models on back order were new products in the line. New products introduced during the current year numbered 192, whereas the total line was 1,150. Another factor to consider was that 374 of the 1,150 products accounted for 90 percent of total sales (34 percent of the products equaled 90 percent of sales). This is not unusual, however; it indicated that perhaps 35 to 55 percent of the present low-volume items were in the line merely to complement the sales of other items. This measure can be costly in terms of additional inventory carrying costs.

Another important figure brought to management's attention was the *annual* increase of new products in the total line. Just three years earlier,

40 percent of all items brought in 90 percent of the sales dollars. This year's total represented a steady 6-percent increase in new products, with no relative decrease in models dropped from the line. A continuing, negative effect on profits remained, because the company was required by the federal government to stock parts for a product for up to seven years after the product was discontinued. Thus every new model in the product line carried a costly inventory burden.

The introduction of new products must be evaluated systematically. The impression I gathered was that Widgets had a strong new-products manager with a highly supportive marketing vice-president. They believed that the more products put in the line, the greater the sales potential was. Because they viewed sales volume as increasing profits, new products seemed to be the route to success. One problem, among many, associated with this view, however, was the lack of new-product evaluation, something that should have been conducted by responsible people.

Widgets was not so big that it could afford the employee hours needed to evaluate 192 new products every year, a rate of about three and a half products per week. With the uncertain sales of new products, how could the company expect to carefully analyze this many new models? They could not.

Listed below are some of the requirements for introducing each new product:

1. Calculations of demand, based on the history of similar products
2. Production runs analysis by product.
3. Production scheduling and procurement
4. Tooling requirements for new products.
5. Updating of the trade repair department inventories
6. Preparation of advertising and other promotions, catalogs, and so on.

It was obvious that the line of new products at the Widget Company was grossly overextended and that the company could not meet its sales forecasts or production estimates. Over the past three years, new products increased from 88 new models to 112 to 192 (16.7% of the total number of products in the line). For the company to continue at this pace, with the already recognized high back-order problem and the danger of low demand for the new product, would be disastrous.

Sales Promotion

Companies sometimes find themselves in an unbalanced position, in that one part of the organization becomes overly dominant. I've seen accountants move a once-strong purchasing department into the production area of a company. I've seen companies so top heavy in production that two production managers were doing the same job. Widget was a sales-dominated company.

We have just seen how new products were overextended. Now let's review the sales promotion program at Widget to determine, among other things, how the company was affected by the new products push.

You will recall the salesman at Retsky's. In addition to having 36 back orders on a single purchase, Retsky claimed that its Graduation program products had not arrived until three months *after* the start of the promotion.

This practice was not uncommon at Widgets. My research, as well as the intercompany correspondence between departments, clarified the problem somewhat. Promotion after promotion was put through the physical distribution system, and each promotion consistently missed its market by three months. Missing the target date of a sales promotion is costly both in terms of employee time and planning and cash dollars invested.

The process of conducting a sales promotion begins with the selection of products that match the theme of the promotion. Either established or new products will be marketed. From this point on, you have two fronts that must be managed: marketing responsibilities and production scheduling. Each represents an important share of cash dollars expended for promotion. Listed below are some of the things that must be done to produce a successful sales promotion:

Marketing responsibilities
—select the product

—make printing preparations for such items as brochures and catalog inserts

—field salespersons market the promotion package

—acquire customer participation in the project; have customers absorb local advertising costs and arrange point-of-purchase display space for products.

Production scheduling
—account for the bill of materials required

—plan the master schedules for size of runs, establishing order of work and setting time performance

—arrange packaging

—arrange delivery

In the course of conducting the above at the Widget's Company, the overall product scheduling and deliveries consistently fell three months behind. Advertising dollars were squandered, both for the customer and for Widgets marketing employee time, and sales efforts were in vain.

It appeared that the sales promotion employees were there merely to go through the motions of performing their job. They seemed helpless to generate point-of-purchase sales by creating an image for and an interest in the company's product. In the case of the Widgets Company, however, there was a huge vacuum. Talented salespeople did their job, but there was no physical product available to cover the cost of advertising and promotion. Because this was done consistently for each promotion, the entire sales promotion was reduced to a paper-distributing department void of profit incentive. The department's annual budget was in excess of $750,000.

Production Scheduling

When heavy sales commitments are imposed on a production department in an organization, several production factors can be affected in important ways—for example, production capacity, production efficiency, performance, and product flow. An overload on any of these areas can have grave consequences, but will certainly have an impact on back orders and cash operations profits.

Production capacity. If there is not enough equipment to meet sales commitments, sales must be cut back. This is only realistic. The other approach is to increase production by expanding facilities.

Expansion of facilities is a broad area for decision analysis. Unfortunately, such decisions are to some degree affected by the national economy. Management usually stops expanding in times of recession and builds during times of growth. In cash operations management, expansion is not the answer to serious internal problems. Quite the contrary. My theory is that companies do not need more sales; they need to take care of those they already have. Corporate expansion should depend on the current yield of corporate profits.

Production efficiency. Included in the term *production efficiency* are two important functions: purchasing efficiency and manufacturing efficiency. A company needs both in its production cycle.

Performance. Is your company pushing too hard to get products out to customers? The Widget Company was sending out reject products with price stickers from dissatisfied customers. What internal problem had caused this situation? Increasing plant capacity won't solve this problem; it will only compound it.

Product flow. Product flow is the area in which good production scheduling and cash planning go hand in hand. Large amounts of cash flow through the production cycle during manufacturing—in materials, money costs, employee time, and overhead. Although back orders are a major problem, if Purchasing is ahead of the production line by two or three months, there is a cost factor of inventory stock shelf costs to consider in cash operations.

Only a small number of problems are mentioned above. In reality, they are symptomatic of larger problems underneath. If the management of the Widgets Company, or of any company in a similar situation, intends to stay on top of a surging marketing thrust, they must understand good management planning as it affects part of a business organization. Production scheduling is not exempt; it must be included in the customer service back-order profit picture.

Inventory Control

Physical Distribution

The months-end back-order report was run off the computers and distributed to the warehouse offices across the country. A day or two passed before the usual phone calls began. Atlanta needed numerous products, to be shipped immediately. Los Angeles, Dallas, and Philadelphia needed similar products for their inventory. The back-order report showed the products as out of stock, and customers were complaining about slow deliveries.

"You have 10,275 of the PT-1226 units there at the central warehouse, for example," the plant manager complained. "Here in L.A. I have a back order for 1,300 units. That's a $4,000 back order on one part. What hurts is that the part is already produced, just sitting in stock. When are your people at the home office going to fix this problem? It happens every month."

The plant manager's point was well taken. Here is how the quantities appeared on the report:

Distribution	Part PT=1226	
Centers	*Inventory*	*Back Orders*
central warehouse	10,275	none
Atlanta	none	442
Dallas	1,905	none
Los Angeles	none	1,278
Philadelphia	847	none
total quantity	13,027	1,720
total dollars	$40,384	$5,332

Notice that Dallas and Philadelphia each had a supply of PT-1226 widgets; therefore, they had no back orders. Atlanta and Los Angeles, however, had no product in stock, so they had $5,332 in back-ordered items. At this same time, $31,853 (10,275 units) were in stock at the central warehouse—early in the month—but the widgets had not been distributed to Dallas and Los Angeles. Why?

We knew there were two problem areas in the physical distribution system that were contributing to back orders: (1) production stock-out and (2) physical handling of the product through distribution. In the case of the PT-1226 widgets, the latter was involved.

The surprising thing about the handling problem was that 75.8% of the back-order models had inventory available at the other distribution centers. The same was true for as many as 340 of 450 back-order models. The problem was clearly widespread.

The fact that the products were in the wrong warehouses was the core of the problem. There simply was no system, manual or mechanized, with which to control the inventory stock-outs at the warehouses. The Widgets Company had no item-by-item inventory-control system, no PNP in marketing or distribution. Add this to the problem of customer service deficiencies and you begin to understand the reason for back orders at the Widgets Company.

Production Stock-Out

We already knew that the third-quarter Widget master plan projected a 58-percent inventory reduction. The schedule for August alone called for a 70.8% decrease in production. When production is ignored to this extent, repercussions are bound to occur at the customer-service level of a company.

And they did. We learned that 50 to 60 percent of back-order dollars could be attributed to the company's inefficient approach to inventory control. Obviously, the company had inventory stock-outs, and in high-dollar products, at that.

The key to an effective inventory-control system is knowing when to refill orders for each item and what quantity to order. From our discussion above, it is clear that the procedures and techniques needed to control the production of the Widgets Company's 1,150 products were obsolete. There was no item-by-item inventory control, no PNP in the production capacity versus an inventory-level phase. This resulted in an unbalanced inventory. It appeared that Widgets' outdated inventory system could not achieve the goal of trading inventory cost for back-order cost.

Warehousing Control

On the twenty-seventh of the month I made one of my frequent trips through Widget's production plant. As I was walking along the aisles, I noticed something I had not noticed on my earlier trips. It seemed that in every aisle were stacks of new widgets in sealed boxes, ready to be shipped. The aisles were two city blocks long, and boxes were stacked in them as far as the eye could see. I stopped a lift-truck operator and asked why all these boxes were in the aisles.

"They're the widgets manufactured the last half of the month," the operator said. "Actually, they should have already gone to the warehouse."

"Why *didn't* they go the warehouse?" I asked.

"Because of the monthly cutoff of shipments to the warehouse. The trucks are stopped at midmonth, and the widgets are shipped from here at the central warehouse. It's a problem. They wait to send it all on the last two days of the month. Everybody works overtime until everything is shipped."

My walk back to the main office was long, so I had time to think over what I had just heard. If shipments to the warehouses were being cut off at midmonth, that would stop the bulk shipments and increase freight costs. It would also overload the physical distribution system with a lopsided monthly shipment schedule. Among other things, that would dominate the computers at the end of the month, resulting in significant overtime, not to mention the effect it would have on customer service.

When I reached the office, my interest was high. Immediately I set out to determine how much in additional costs, and what deficiencies, was caused by the decision to stop the mid-month shipments to the warehouses.

The Logic Behind the Mid-Month Cutoffs

My analysis revealed some flaws in the physical distribution system. The interesting thing was that the local management people had approved the cut-off policy.

The cutoff had to do with the company's sales imbalance. The vice-president for marketing talked the division controller into holding the trucks at midmonth (the marketing department dominated the production department). Marketing's idea was to hold all shipments at the central warehouse from the 15th, to the end of the month, add it to the sales from the midmonth point, and declare the total volume as sales for the current month. If the trucks had been released at midmonth, those sales (products), as well as the last half-month's products, would likely miss the current month's sales because they were in transit.

What if management did not use the cutoff? The effect would be that *sales during the first month would be 40 percent lower than anticipated on the financial statements.* The bottom profit line would show red all the way back to corporate headquarters.

In the meantime, cash operations distribution systems and procedures were being rendered useless by cut-off inefficiency. On a month-to-month basis, negative figures were hidden, whereas in the long run, company profits were on a disastrous course.

The cutoff of shipments was essentially a poor business principle. The entire approach had been poor from the start, when the initial reason is considered, of opening expensive warehouses to use them for regional shipments to customers to achieve bulk-freight economies. This practice doomed the plan at the outset. The repercussions were numerous and costly. Let's look at them in two parts—shipment cutoffs to the warehouses, and shipment of 40 percent of the month's sales during the last two days of each month.

Shipment Cutoffs to Warehouses

The key to holding inventory levels of finished goods is a well-planned reorder system. If the foundation of a planned system was undermined, inventory levels would fall and the number of costly back orders would rise.

We knew that the Widgets Company was using an outdated inventory-control system. Therefore, the company could ill afford to engage in off-beat transactions in its inventories. Widgets' management people, however, were too insecure to face a losing month, so they continually pulled this off-beat policy. The price paid was back orders. My analysis indicated that approximately 38 percent of the back orders for the past year, representing a carryover of $4.1 million in back orders, was caused by automatic shipment cutoff of incomplete orders at the warehouses. The situation would continue if warehouse inventory levels were not increased to the proper in-stock level and maintained there for each product in the line.

The practice of cutting off shipments at mid-month was interrupting the monthly shipment cycle at the Widget Company. The widget industry had problems enough with seasonal orders. To compound the problem with internal inefficiency was a serious error.

Forty Percent of Shipments Made during last Two days of the Month

The frustration of a strong monthly order cycle in industry can make it difficult for business organizations. Problems can develop in cash flow, inventory levels, labor, and overhead charges. When these problems are compounded by deliberate interruptions of shipping, something is terribly wrong with management.

The deliberate policy of shipping 40 percent of sales dollars out on the last two days of the month has to be something of a record. It is understood that all companies push to get sales in on the current month's transactions, but generally not more than 10 percent of volume, and even that is high.

Extremities of Processing Costs

Instead of three weeks' delivery from the warehouses, six weeks were required. Can you imagine how many trucks would have to be in line at Widgets' shipping docks on the last two days of each month? The company was sending out $2 million worth of boxed products in two 24-hour periods. There was no way that it could ship that many widgets in two days. The company, could, however, load and move that many trucks by working round the clock. This is what Widget did. Truck drivers drove the trucks to parking lots in nearby towns and "dropped them off." As long as the product was on the truck, it was considered a sale.

This was all the management people needed—a recorded sale. The fact that a shipment was not delivered made no difference on the financial statement. The division controller had done his job. The vice-president for marketing provided the controller with sales orders, and Accounting saw to it that the orders were entered on the financial statements. Now the controller could go back to the *Wall Street Journal.*

The problem of those parked trucks loaded with widgets remained, however. They were spread all over the county. The earliest the truckers could deliver them was in four to six weeks. In the meantime, what was happening to customer service? Here are some of the problems that resulted from shipping on the last two days of the month.

Pressure on Handling Materials. Employees who handled materials were exhausted by the end of each month. In addition, the equipment for labeling, for temporary storage, and for packaging transport—fork lift trucks, pallets, monorails, roller conveyors, and so on—was overloaded. There was no time for moves designed to increase economy or to eliminate bottlenecks, reduce product-travel distance, wastage, and flow lines. The push to get the product out was on, as were charges for overtime. Fifty-three thousand dollars was paid in overtime annually because of the two monthly push days.

Backed-up Computers. The electronic data processing department had a six-month backlog in priority programs and jobs. Near the end of each month, however to take care of the push, EDP was expected to set aside eight to ten days of computer time to process orders, shipments, and invoices, including the month's-end financial statements. This put great pressure on other departments that needed data processing information, inventory statistics, and sales distribution information for field people, and for purchasing totals. The two-day push took a third of the computer's time. It interrupted the flow of business information needed and expected by the other departments. This was another costly operations function that never showed on the company's financial statements.

Additional Freight Costs. We have already seen that there were additional freight costs due to processing 15,000 additional orders over the past year. This problem was related to the monthly cutoff, in that freight rates were 146 percent higher when they were taken off the bulk shipment distribution. When the rates were pulled from the bulk trucks, the products were sent on a single-shipment price and, in many instances, on a minimum-charge shipment. This was related to a shipment that might weigh only three pounds but which was charged a 10-pound minimum price.

Another freight cost factor that did not always appear in the freight-cost column on the statements was storage costs for parking the trucks in nearby towns. These trucks had to be secured since each one contained $30,000 worth of widgets. To protect them properly, the trucks must be placed in a secure parking area, and that storage was expensive. The mode of routing the parked trucks would also change from the central warehouses; thus duplicate papers had to be processed on freight shipping plans. When such changes occur so often in business systems, they are sure to cause costly problems. Freight costs were a problem at the Widgets Company.

Sales Cancellations. Sales cancellations was the costliest problem at Widgets that was related to increased processing costs. When shipments were held on trucks for several weeks after the invoices were sent to customers, unhappy customers resulted. If such a situation continues, the company can lose customers.

Many of Widgets' six-week shipments were back-order replacements. When six weeks is added to the original poor delivery date, the company was bound to suffer sales cancellations.

The cut off of shipments results in two additional costs. When customers cancel they do not accept delivery; thus return freight is charged, plus additional dock costs. The other cost is the cost of money. If finished goods in transit have not reached the customer, the shipper still has money tied up in the products. If $30,000 worth of products is sitting in storage for six weeks, count on another six weeks from processing the product through manufacturing to the ultimate time when cash is received from the customer. If 12 weeks have passed, at 12 percent cost of money, $900 is lost in cash profits—per truckload of widgets.

Order Processing

The best marketing results in a company are obtained through a well-designed sales plan, both in sales aids and with well-trained salespeople. Office staffs should provide salespersons with promotion plans, history, and market trend information. In addition, the company can save time and effort in marketing by planning sales routes, setting sales quotas, analyzing sales performance, and developing sales cost analysis for salespeople. Next come the integral parts of advertising and promotion: discovering the advertising appeal of the product and reasons for buying it.

Customer service people must assist by answering customers inquiries, handling mail and telephone orders, setting delivery dates, and giving leads to salespeople. Most important, they must see that orders are processed as efficiently as possible.

Widgets Manufacturing Company of America was using all the right principles. Every part of the marketing system was functioning or was capable of meeting the responsibilities expected of it. It had one big problem, however. Despite its preparation and good intentions, Marketing was not performing properly. Why? Because the company was not delivering the product on time.

The problem was not that Widget could not produce the product but that management had adopted a poor distribution procedure for the product. Following is a review of management's mistakes as they were found by the COM program. Management:

purposely decreased production of finished goods inventories on the master plan

cut off shipments to the warehouses at mid-month, knocking inventory levels out of balance

promoted new products beyond production capabilities

often reduced production levels below sales forecasts

ignored profitable systems and procedures in favor of company politics

held 40 percent of sales for shipment on the last two days of each month, disrupting the monthly shipment cycle

These mistakes were detrimental to profits, in that they were repetitive by structure, on a month-to-month basis. Because of these mistakes, the company's systems were disrupted. The problems would not solve themselves; instead, the current problems were being compounded by the failure to adopt good systems and procedures.

Profit and Loss in Early Shipments

In business, one problem can often lead to another. As an example, let's look at a problem related to the one above, a problem that had to do with early shipments.

Over a period of several months I noticed, in my review, a disregard for *specified* shipping dates on orders. Orders were being deliberately moved forward so that sales dollars could be recorded in the preceding month. Not only was management reaching into the first two days of the next month to improve the current month's sales picture, they were also shipping orders that were not due for shipment in order to obtain sales volume.

Sending products to customers earlier than projected can cause surprising cash profit losses. This procedure is both expensive and risky in terms of customer relations. Here are some expense items:

Storage charges at the freight terminal during the notification period, starting with the point at which the customer refuses the merchandise

Additional storage charges when a company chooses to leave merchandise at the freight company until the date on which it can be delivered

Redelivery charges from the freight company to the customer

Cost of freight back to the shipping point if the merchandise cannot be stored at the trucker's terminal or if management decided not to return it because of excessive storage costs

Cost of reshipping on the specified date

Cost of the time it takes for company employees to make decisions on all of the above

A big risk involved here is the loss of the freight carrier's liability. The carrier is not liable for merchandise on the dock or in storage. Liability covers merchandise only while it is in transit.

The last point to be made here concerns occasional irritation on the part of the customer. When a product is shipped and the customer is invoiced early, the customer is not prepared to handle the receipt or to process the paperwork involved in shipment. This can cause time-consuming problems and errors that will eventually have to be resolved.

One other point should be noted. An annual profit loss of $120,000 was directly tied to the aforementioned early shipment. This loss had escaped detection by the company's systems and procedures.

The Truck Strike Fiasco

While we are on the subject of chain-reaction errors, let us review another problem at the Widgets Company that developed as a result of shipment on the last two days of the month. One of the most widespread and protracted truck strikes began soon after the first of a particular month. Because Widget's management people saw it coming, they prepared for the strike. Widget inventories were increased. With five days to go until the end of the month, the trucks were brought to the loading docks.

Trucks were virtually hijacked, as many as could be found so that the company could beat the month's-end push before the strike began. Trailer after trailer was filled with widgets; as many as 65 trucks were on the move. Then a truck strike was called.

The management and customer service people at Widgets had not anticipated the impact of their mistake until the phone calls began, saying that widgets had not arrived. The truck strike brought everything to a halt. Practically all of the widgets trucks were in storage lots. Some trucks were not found for 6 to 10 months; others were never found.

The losses multiplied. Additional employee functions and costs included extra paperwork, location of trucks (teams of office workers were sent cross-country to parking areas off the trucking routes), reshipment to customers, wages to additional employees, the cost of money, sales cancellations, and, costliest of all, lost products in the missing trucks. An accurate count was never made; cash losses, however, were estimated at more than $1 million. Some employees said that the loss was closer to $3 million. The damage done to customer relations was immeasurable.

Advertising and Promotion

The idea in advertising and sales promotion is to stimulate interest about certain models in the product line over a specific period of time. The deficiencies and idiosyncrasies of Widget's physical distribution system hindered achievement of the company's sales goals.

Advertising and promotion are intended to increase demand and augment the sale of products and/or services. When the cash operations management of these areas becomes inefficient, direct cash losses occur.

Quality Control

Let's refer again to the Kansas City salesman who was summoned to the offices of a customer to be told about the customer receiving reject products. The customer's products carried price stickers that indicated they were rejects sent back from a prior customer.

This type of marketing deficiency reveals breakdown in quality control or that inadequate procedures are being followed that affect the system outside quality control. My analysis in this area brought out some interesting points on the technical and economic standards of quality control at the Widget Company. Here are some of the factors involved in customer dissatisfaction:

There had been a 43-percent cutback in the number of quality-control employees. Inevitably, quality control suffered the most from the cutback. It was the expendable department in terms of overhead.

Only a half day's inspection was alloted to the three assembly-line machines that did most of the production. These machines had a 40-percent reject history 20 to 50 percent of the time. The lines required a full day's inspection.

Only one 8-hour shift was pulled in final inspection on the 24-hour month's-end shipping days. Thus, of the 40 percent of products shipped on the last two days, two-thirds were never inspected.

Reducing quality control operations will directly affect the reject rate, as well as increase the number of units to be repaired. Problems arose in this area in correlation to the number of back orders. Instead of backlog of two to three weeks, the company experienced a trade-repair backlog of seven to nine weeks.

In some instances, repair employees were switched to production. Occasionally, management sent specific rush orders to repair to expedite shipments to unhappy customers. Again, this interrupted the flow from production.

Conclusions and Recommendations

In the COM customer service review for the Widget Company, the entire physical distribution system was reviewed. The areas of physical distribution covered the complete cycle; orders, invoicing, and materials flow through Widget. The following functions were analyzed: (1) sales forecasting, (2) production scheduling, (3) inventory control, (4) order processing, (5) warehousing control, (6) quality control, and (7) advertising and promotion.

I observed in my research that customer service was, indeed, at a low level. This was confirmed, first, by the discovery of the excessive processing costs that were occurring in systems and procedures (a $1.3 million annual loss), and second, by the discovery of operations problems caused by an inefficient physical distribution system.

In my final report to management, I pointed out the excessive processing costs and made recommendations for improving the level of customer service. The estimated amount of potential, increased gross profits was estimated at $1.8 to $3.5 million annually.

Sales Forecasting, Production Scheduling and Inventory Control

The key to good inventory control is knowing what is happening in the inventory through item-by-item calculations. Stock-out inventory levels cannot be improved unless there is a balanced knowledge of the product history of each item in inventory.

There is an economic trade-off between finished-goods inventory control and inventory shelf costs and good customer service. Back orders could be virtually eliminated if inventories of finished goods had no quantity limits. But this, of course, is not economically feasible. Each inventory item must be brought to a trade-off balance—to the part number principle (PNP).

We saw in chapter 4 that PNP is usually identified as a combination of advanced inventory control and *usage* control. The same format is needed here, for a short-term, finished-goods inventory control—only in reverse.

Instead of product usage, in marketing we think of product demand. What does the customer need (sales forecast)? What is the customer's average order size? Is the product on the shelf (shelf cost)? What value is placed on the inventory item? Can you carry that much cash on the shelf? How soon can the product be produced (production lead time or purchase lead time)? Once you have the answers to these questions for each item, the trade-off can be calculated item by item. *This is the key to proper finished-goods inventory control.* When this key escapes your company's system, you have lost control to big cash profits in material flow—below the cash management level-line.

To acquire control is not easy. This was especially true of the Widget Company. Widget's carried 1,150 products in its product line. To get a count of all its products, the company had to turn to a computer. Since the computer already carried an item-by-item sales distribution history, an automated physical distribution system could be adapted. Extended interest and capable management, however, would be needed to implement an effective, sophisticated, distribution control system.

Order Processing

Once the part number principle is applied to the inventory of finished goods, customer service levels will respond even to relatively small changes in inventory. This may be surprising, but several such short-term projects should result in immediate improvements in the system.

An example is the systems review discussed above in this chapter, where I state that 75.8% of back-order items were sufficiently stocked in the warehouses. This implies that we need only administer the PNP to the back-order items (restoring item-by-item control) to gain control of warehouse inventories, with little cash investment. The analysis done and the technical improvements made in the system require little concentrated effort. But it headed the Widgets Company in the right direction.

Shipment Cutoffs to Warehouses

One recommendation for improving customer service at the Widget Company was to make a minor change in procedures. The company must ship to the warehouses throughout the month. That would support inventory levels and sustain present sales forecasts. Both would contribute admirably to an immediate, short-term answer for improved customer service and inventory of finished goods. This is a relatively minor change for the systems to handle, but it will yield significant improvements in stock control, as well as cash savings in distribution-processing costs.

Replenish Master-Plan Quantities

The production master plan is a guide to controlling inventory levels during production. When the plan is abused through deliberate inventory reduction below sales forecast, a penalty will be paid in the form of stock-outs.

Because customer service is affected by limited production, my recommendation was to extend lead times with greater inventories of finished goods; at the same time, I cautioned restraint in these extensions. Processing methods could be improved through production lead time and purchasing procedures by breaking down material requirements on an item-by-item basis. This requires a moderate increase in inventory costs while making possible the maintenance of efficient inventory level.

Smooth Out the Monthly Shipment Cycle

A strong monthly shipment cycle existed, which greatly disturbed the order flow in customer service. This entailed shipping 40 percent of the units ordered on the last two days of each month. The problem affected customer delivery, put pressure on material handling, backed up the computers in schedule, caused additional freight costs and, worst of all, increased cancellation of orders.

My recommendation of discontinuing shipment cutoffs at midmonth was the answer for this problem, too. Considerable improvements in efficiency would result by spreading shipments throughout the month to smooth the monthly shipment cycle.

New Products

Problems in distribution are related directly to the number of items in the product line. The Widgets Company carried a large number of slow sellers in its line. This was concluded when it was noticed that 34 percent of the items in the product line accounted for 90 percent of sales. One significant part of this unbalanced product line had to do with the increasing number of new products.

We determined in our analysis of new products that the company had overextended itself in introducing new models into the line on an annual basis. Therefore, in conjunction with instituting improvements in the distribution system, I recommended a product review of each low-volume model in the line to determine its value in the marketing system.

The review was to be based on such factors as sales distribution history, future potential, back-order data, production lead times, profit margin, and requirement to make up assemblies. Products that showed no movement, or that showed little contribution to the overall sales program, were recommended for removal from the line.

From the same perspective, future introductions of new products should be systematically evaluated. Management should give careful consideration to slowing down new-product promotion in favor of operations improvement through inventory control in the physical distribution system. Improved forecasting methods should be sought for all product lines.

Sales Promotion

The Widget Company's sales promotions missed target dates for delivery of products. Decision analysis was recommended for all future promotions. Factors included were production capability, capacity constraints, frequency patterns of promotions, new-product promotions, improved forecasting methods, and degree of customer satisfaction expected. Breaking this down, my suggestion was to reduce the number of sales promotions (advertising costs) until the production department and the physical distributions area could facilitate product requirements.

Warehousing

Many of the warehousing troublespots will be improved by implementation of the above recommendations. This includes improvement of back orders and sales cancellations through (1) a stop on mid-month shipment cutoffs, and (2) discontinuance of shipping 40 percent of sales on the last two days of the month. By applying detailed (item-by-item) inventory control and improving the quantities called for in the master plan, warehousing distribution would be greatly improved. Smoothing the product flow through long-term decision analysis should be applicable only for optimal distribution performance, which would be recommended sometime in the distant future.

Warehousing process costs, however, is another expense factor to be reconciled with cash-profit improvement. Recommendations were made for dispensing with the cost-per-dollar-shipped basis for payment of warehousing costs in favor of total square-footage rental or ownership. This was based on the Widgets Company's ability to put greater sales-dollar volume through the dollar-shipped-based warehouses. I also suggested that management consider the relocation of warehouses that are charged an annual floor tax, in favor of locations in states that do not charge this tax.

Quality Control, Advertising, and Promotion

The area of quality control is important in the physical distribution system of a business, both technically and economically. The more technical the product, the stronger the reason for quality control.

The Widgets product was sensitive in regard to quality for customer satisfaction. The company needed an active delivery response in order to have an advertising impact and achieve lasting, quality performance. This would require an efficient marketing program for physical distribution. To do this—and increase quality control at the same time—my recommendation to the Widgets Company was to rebuild the quality control staff to a standard of effective control to ensure uniform product quality. Decision analysis would be used to determine how much inspection would be needed in the future.

Summary

Customer service was judged to be at an all-time low level at the Widgets Company. This had caused enormous profit losses through systems fluctuations and processing costs.

Deficiencies in the physical distribution system resulted in an excess of back orders and cancellation of orders. The deficiencies were traced to two product-control areas: production-inventory control and physical distribution. The main causes of the back-order and order-cancellation deficiencies were evaluated on the basis of both the number of back-order items in the product line and the dollar value of back orders. The primary deficiencies that caused the back orders were: (1) no specific item-by-item inventory analysis, (2) a strong monthly shipment cycle, (3) midmonth shipment cutoffs to the warehouses, (4) master plan inventories below sales forecasts, (5) a substandard level of quality control, and (6) the promotion of new products beyond production capabilities.

All of the above are the province of cash operations management. As was mentioned, the cash-dollar losses were occurring because of incremental processing costs. In addition, poor customer service was causing systems losses estimated at $1.8 and $3.5 million annually.

My recommendations to Widget Manufacturing Company of America concerned the development of short-term cash management changes that would offer substantial customer service benefits through operations.

These changes would yield a quick solution that would solve much of the present customer service problem. The adjustments could be made immediately by Widget personnel or through my consultant service.

A long-term approach was also suggested, which would yield further improvements but required more time and effort for completion. Such an approach was intended for a permanent, more balanced product distribution. Included in the long-term recommendations were, first, to systematically drop at least 500 models from the product line. This represented perhaps 5 percent of total sales but would reduce product-quantity responsibility to a more manageable inventory level.

Another recommendation was to design an automated distribution program for the purpose of identifying inventory problems at an early stage, so that inventory levels may be replenished in time to meet shipping dates.

The effect of these recommendations was expected to bring the Widgets Company to a high level of customer service and to increase efficiency.

For a long-term solution, in-depth inventory calculations would be used, including a study of distribution variables, cost-effectiveness curves, and so on, to establish a standard for cost and control policies.

Questions on Chapter 11

CUSTOMER SERVICE

1. Does your company have a multiproduct sales division that depends on manual, physical-distribution decisions? If so, do you have problems similar to those of the Widgets Company?
2. What percentage of the products in your company's sales line makes up the greatest percentage of sales? By units? By dollars?
3. Should you be concerned about a back-order situation in your company?
4. Have you analyzed your customer service level improvement possibilities during the past 12 months? The past 24 months?
5. Have you conducted analyses of physical distribution processing costs during the past 12 months?
6. What would you estimate as the cost of processing a sales invoice and order through your distribution system?
7. Have you analyzed samples of orders for order-completion dates to determine whether you have a serious distribution problem?
8. Have you noticed significant fluctuations in freight costs during the past 12 months compared with the previous two 12-month periods?

9. What level have sales cancellations maintained during the past 12 months compared with the previous two 12-month periods?
10. Have customer returns fluctuated seriously over the past 12 months? The past 24 months?
11. What cost structure is your company using for warehousing? Do you own? Rent? What is the per-dollar shipped volume?
12. Do you foresee possible improvements in your warehouse costs by making a change in your cost structure?

SALES FORECASTING

13. Has your production department maintained a consistent inventory level to meet sales forecasts consistently over the past 12 months?
14. Are you aware of the repercussions if inventory and production demands do not meet the product goals set forth in the master plan?
15. Have you automated your flow of production by planning procurement and production? Do your employees react quickly to decision changes in this area?
16. Are new products systematically evaluated to your satisfaction?
17. What percentage of your product line is composed of new products?
18. Have you checked with your tooling department for ideas about how new products perform?
19. Are new products a problem in your company? A significant part?
20. Are your company's sales promotions hitting their target dates?
21. What advertising dollar agreements are worked out with your customers on sales promotions?
22. Do the number of annual sales promotions seem appropriate for your company's production capacity?
23. What four factors apply to the production department's ability to meet sales commitments and requirements?
24. What is an appropriate guideline for corporate expansion?
25. Do you detect a departmental dominance thrust by any department? Do you foresee negative profit elements developing from such a thrust?
26. Are your company warehouses supplied commensurate with product distribution?
27. Do you recognize inventory problems due to shortages, which may contribute to a back-order problem?
28. Do you see any similarities between your warehouse distribution systems and those at the Widget company?
29. Does your company utilize item-by-item inventory control in your distribution system? Manual or automated?
30. Are your production capabilities in line with sales forecasts?

31. Are master plan production inventory levels respected by your management people?
32. Does your company ship too many orders near the end of each month?
33. Have you run an analysis to determine what proportion of additional processing costs are caused by overloads?
34. What repercussions in processing functions and costs may result from overloads? What areas of your business are affected?

ORDER PROCESSING

35. Are your company's products on a precise delivery schedule?
36. Does your company ship orders ahead of scheduled delivery dates?
37. Have delivery policies been analyzed recently for possible improvement?
38. What is the dollar amount appropriated for sales promotion in your company (separate from direct advertising dollars)?
39. Do your standards of quality control complement your customer service?
40. Are parts inventories in your repair department sufficient to meet demand?
41. What are the seven main functions of distribution in a production-and-distribution business organization?

12. CPAs, Accountants, and the Profit Person

Throughout my years studying business operations, I have looked for the person responsible for maintaining the efficiency of an organization. I have looked for the profit person, the person who cares whether the company makes a profit, the person who cares about job efficiency. To find that person is often difficult. Employees who I think have that responsibility are nowhere to be found when I go looking for them.

The thought that is always before me is, who is checking on the efficiency of the company's operations?

As I have mentioned, an employee is usually not given the opportunity to complete all the work that must be done in that employee's area of responsibility. If this is always true, then no employee is checking efficiency.

This brings me to an engrossing business point. If employees do not check on company operations, who does? You will often hear the answer when the question comes up. The answer is, the accountants—if not outside accountants (CPAs) then inside accountants.

Somewhere along the way, corporation employees have developed an erroneous picture of who controls profit efficiencies in business organizations. I do not accept the notion that accountants are the profit-makers. Nor do I accept the theory that accountants are directly responsible for cash operations profits and losses.

What is behind this belief that accountants are the profit people in a company? Do outside accountants set the standards that guide company systems and procedures? This chapter is devoted to that subject. My intention is to fill in another piece of the business person's puzzle, to explain the part accountants play in bringing profits to a business organization through cash operations management.

The approach taken is to disclose the responsibilities and characteristics of the CPA, the company accountant, and the profit person, to determine where each one stands in a company's profit picture.

The CPA

The Big 8 are the eight largest certified public accounting firms in the United States. The are the elite of the accounting profession, the best money can buy.

I have spent many working hours with people from these firms and have the highest professional regard for them and their firms. Not only do they exhibit great interest in their clients' businesses, they also offer a personable approach to the employees in their clients' offices.

My only regret about CPA firms is that theirs, it would appear, is a worthless cause. Their use of highly trained people to double-check (audit) corporate financial statements is a massive waste of talent.

The Big-8 firms are limited. They are limited in the recommendations they can make. They are limited by the fact that they must charge large fees to cover their high overhead, overhead that puts costs out of reach for some clients who need the benefit of their expertise. They are limited in how much assistance they can give clients, because the external audit is not timely enough to offer profit-improvement suggestions for stopping cash losses in systems and procedures. As matters stand, the large CPA firms offer only this: "In accordance with generally accepted auditing standards . . . . In our opinion, the financial statements referred to present fairly the financial position of _____ Company, in conformity with generally accepted accounting principles."

Who Are the CPAs?

A recruiting specialist from a leading CPA firm was talking with a top graduate during a coffee break at a management recruiting session at a major American university. The session was attended by several Big 8 firms, as well as numerous selected graduates from that year's graduating class. It was a premier event for the graduates.

Abruptly a recruiter from a competing CPA firm moved between the two. "I would like you to consider my firm for prospective employment," he said, intruding in the conversation. He slipped a business card into the graduate's hand, took the graduate by the shoulder, and walked him away, all the while explaining the advancement potential at the recruiter's firm.

This is not an uncommon occurrence. The Big 8 recruiters are under instructions to get the top graduates to sign up with *their* firm.

The CPA has become stereotyped as a studious introvert with a bland personality. There may still be some of those around today, but over the years this image has altered greatly. Today's Big 8 CPA is in no way an introvert. He or she is only one in a crowd who appear studious but not bland. They remain cautious and conservative, but their intellects and range of knowledge and information place them among their peers in any professional field.

They are not, however, infalliable. As is true of other professions, there is a wide range of competency and endurance among the individual CPAs. Let's follow the careers of three CPA acquaintances of mine to try to find out what a CPA is.

The first of the CPA professionals choose not to compete for a partnership in his firm. Instead, he selected a controller position in a small, struggling company on the outskirts of Chicago. The second CPA failed to qualify for a partnership but was appointed as corporate controller in a large company, heading up 15 divisions. Both joined previous clients and both were, at the time, 34 years old. The third CPA stayed with his firm and went for a partnership.

A couple of years passed. I stayed in touch with these CPAs and watched their progress. The first CPA was a model of success. He progressed to the position of executive vice-president. He earned and was given full authority for improving his small company. "Jerry," he said, "we decreased our labor wages more than we increased our sales in the past two years. I guess that's not saying much for our sales," he added, quickly.

He needn't have been so apologetic. His words and working standards told me vividly that he was a profit person. Thousands of business executives in commerce and industry would love to have his capacity for business techniques. Also, I can't say enough about restraint of sales to acquire profits through cost improvements.

The second CPA, the corporate controller of the 15 divisions of a large company, was found in his office one day behind closed doors shaking his head and mumbling to himself. He had taken on too much too soon. It seemed that profits and systems at one of his divisions had gone sour, compounding his other problems. I later heard that he moved his family back to his hometown in Kansas, where, in time, he probably succeeded.

The third CPA was a "country bumpkin" raised in central Illinois. Whatever drawbacks his rural upbringing caused, they were apparently left behind. He was a smooth, flamboyant, lady's man, a likeable, personable CPA. He had one goal: to be a top CPA. Effortlessly, it seemed, he has climbed the final steps to a Big-8 partnership.

The Audit: For Certification or Profit?

The work, planning, and expertise that CPAs put into their external audit programs are developed from a well-composed master plan. The work papers, checkpoints, percentages, and check marks all fit into an organized, professional approach that performs wonderfully on the business books of corporations.

What is the purpose of their work? Let me elaborate on my comment above that I felt their external audits are conducted for a worthless cause. I am a profit person. Therefore, I should not have a liberal bone in my body. Of course, such a viewpoint makes it difficult for me to accept costly business projects that are potentially useless. When a client pays $175,000 for an outside CPA audit, just to double-check the client's already accurate accounting records, and when no check is made on the operating efficiency of the company, it inevitably disturbs my conservative patterns.

Here is an example of an audit performed for a client if mine. As the audit got underway, the firm worked a task force of at least five CPAs hour after hour, plus overtime, to prove general ledger balances. In addition, my client had its own accounting staff, working on the audit, as well as outside part-time accountants, not to mention the rented calculators they needed to keep going. The audit team verified that the assets and liabilities of the company were:

1,650	production machines	= fixed assets
$16,672,000	inventory	= assets
7,600,000	receivables (10% bad)	= assets
336,000	cash	= assets
5,275,000	payables	= liabilities
13,000,000	loans	= liabilities
total for certification		= net worth

The audit issued from the CPA office revealed that inventory counts were conducted properly, that accounts receivable were overextended, that accounts payable were underextended. The fee for the audit was $175,000. The certified audit report was sent to the company stockholders, —as a "bloated cow" on its way to market.

Now what brought on this comment? There is a reason. At the time these auditors were hovering over my client's books, my COM program was in progress. While the signed CPA certification was on its way to the stockholders, I had uncovered hundreds of thousands of lost dollars that had been ignored in the CPA audit—money that had slipped below the cash management level-line, through the hands of the accountants.

What significance does a financial statement offer stockholders when it excludes $2 million in internal losses evading the company's systems annually? If the company reports a $3.5 million gross profit but has the potential of adding another $2 million gross, wouldn't this information be important to stockholders? In this case, the $2 million in losses was known by management weeks before the statements were issued, but the auditors did not know. Wouldn't such facts make the audit report questionable?

Review of a second audit

You will recall that in Chapter 5 we discussed cash payment policies. There, too, an external audit was conducted just before a COM program, and additional profits were disclosed that had been overlooked by the CPAs.

In our study we found that $100,000 was lost because $2 million was paid in advance, consistently, for every payables pay period. Let's follow up on the audit.

An important part of a CPA audit is to conduct a price test on products in the raw materials inventory. If prices on inventory values match the actual prices paid on vendor invoices, the test is complete and inventory values are considered valid. To conduct this test the auditors select samples of high-value parts in the inventory. Next, they locate names of vendors who supply the parts and select three of their invoices for price sampling. The invoices are listed on column spread sheets under specific headings as follows: invoice date, amount, quantity, unit price, terms of payment, and date of payment.

Now, what do we see? Along with price information, the audit provides date information that indicates when the invoices were paid. The auditors wanted the dates for "inventory aging" purposes and to establish a credit rating. The fact that the invoices had been paid too soon was not part of their test, but the dates were, and they said something.

There was another intriguing aspect of this audit. It concerned my familiarity with the facts. I had personally handled this audit price test for the CPAs.

The emphasis in Chapter 5 is on the COM program, which can be used to discover profit loss. In using the program we concentrate on total dollars and search for deficiencies. The purpose of the CPA test, however, was to prove inventory values and aging. No efficiency checks were included; the auditors were interested in "certification." It seems the drift of what the auditors were saying about payments was, "By paying these invoices before the 30 days were up, the client earned a good credit rating." This was true. But the client did have a $100,000 efficiency problem. Even I missed it, using the CPA external audit procedures.

The Purpose: Audit and Cash Operations Management

We have covered the subject fairly well, well enough not to have lost our perspective, I hope. The million-dollar profits mentioned in the example above was in "operations" dollars picked up by the COM profit-efficiency program. The objectives of this program are to assist business people by improving operational efficiency within an organization.

The CPA external audit has a different purpose. That purpose is verification and certification of the financial records and statements of the company, keeping in mind the stockholders and government regulations. The external audit is not designed to stop million-dollar losses. It is intended merely to verify the financial standing of the company on the basis of the company's accounting records.

The Need for CPAs

Much of the United States' CPA talent seems to be pointed in the wrong direction. Industrial and commercial companies need CPAs to audit their profit-efficiency programs. Auditors are needed to keep an eye on government spending. The economy needs monitoring. All these areas can be improved by making better use of CPAs.

We must do more to bring good CPAs into the business-efficiency areas in industry. CPAs are trained to be good business organizers. More important, they are acquainted with the principles of operations business management. They know what a good inventory turnover can do for a company, and how to use a return-on-investment factor to measure effectiveness in every part of the organization. They will dig in to prove their point. When it comes to profit-dollar business, CPAs give direct answers and point to specific causes. In short, they are good "profit people."

Business and government must include CPAs more fully in their efficiency decision. CPAs are expensive, but look at the problem another way. Your excessive operations costs will be compounded if you don't hire them.

The Accountant

I walked into the office of the financial vice-president and laid a copy of my COM proposal on his desk. I had just completed a preliminary review. The time had come to put the vice-president's COM profit program in action.

The preliminary program had been highly successful. The amount of cash recovery had already reached and passed $100,000; improvements in systems and procedures would yield another $300,000 annually, and probably more. The COM program would triple prior cash recovery. Total improvements in the proposal would increase the vice-president's profits by a margin of 35 percent.

In the proposal I suggested that the client assign a team, a task force, to me temporarily to conduct a 2,000-hour COM profit program.

"Jerry," the vice-president said, "we've done some thinking on the subject. We certainly thank you for the good work you've done for our company, but now we feel we can do this work ourselves. We are going to turn the program over to our accountants." This shortsighted business-management decision cost that small company more than $500,000 in lost profits over the next 12 months.

As is true of most accounting departments, the accountants in the company were not prepared to handle a profit-improvement program. The primary reason was that the accountants were not profit persons; they were accountants.

This new assignment, the COM program, required several ambitious profit people. An accountant who is not a profit person is not as likely to check efficiencies in the accounting area of a company. This also applies to engineers, purchasing agents, and marketing service managers. If they aren't checking efficiency, they are not profit people. They are more likely to confine themselves to the procedural responsibilities implied by their titles.

The profit person in an organization is that rare employee who applies profits and procedures to improve efficiency to every part of a job. The profit person has that additional ability to convince management to take a positive approach to profits in business operations.

Why Couldn't Accountants Handle a COM Program?

Why couldn't the accountants of the company under discussion take on the added commitment of a COM program? There were several reasons why they couldn't. They were not profit conscious. There were other reasons, however.

Accountants have numerous responsibilities. They have jobs to complete that are of prime interest to top management. For instance, if the president and the vice-presidents do not receive a financial statement at the end of the month, all hell breaks loose. Without a doubt, the accountants will take five, or maybe ten days, out of their 22-day work month to prepare financial statements. This is one-third of their work time, all of it spent on clerical accumulation and organization of accounting statistics. None of it can be applied to improving cash operations management profits.

Another accounting responsibility is to assist CPAs in external audits. These audits, as I said, are not related to profits.

The EDP department can be a thorn in the accountant's side, particularly if EDP is under the financial wing of the company. Accounting is primarily responsible for regulations, and cash flow. Then come the daily responsibilities of entries to the general ledger, payables, receivables, credit functions, and payroll, not to mention employee problems, turnover, training, and organization. Then there are numerous special projects, bond issues, dividend payments, taxes—or a complete general ledger to be rewritten for computer application.

Under these circumstances, it is not hard to see why it is difficult to fit a COM profit program into an office's already congested accounting schedule, into an environment oriented toward financial systems and procedures. The accountants are seldom operations-oriented. Their business instincts and interests are financial. That is all companies should expect from their accountants: to work up and present a good set of accounting records. Let the management people—who should be profit persons—take it from there. Make the accountants responsible only for financial services. Hire operations people to supply management with analyses of operations. Do not expect your accountants to do this work unless they have plenty of extra time.

Below are some reasons why accountants should not be expected to carry the cash-operations analysis load of a company.

1. Accountants are not operations profit people. They are financial records and systems people. The two areas are far apart when it comes to earning operations profits. Accounting responsibilities lie in the subject areas, general ledgers, CPA audits, EDP, taxes, and cash flow, none of which touches cash operations profits. These are financial services performed for the company. The operations profit person will use these financial services to pinpoint additional profits.

2. Operations profits do not rate high among accountants' priorities within a company. Most of the time, these profits rank lowest. One reason is a corporation's hierarchy pressures and priority customs. The general ledger ranks the highest. Why? Because it is prepared for top management. The general ledger is used to produce financial statements. Apparently, if the accountants provide a good financial statement, their main responsibility has been met for the month. The gratuities increase when the accountants can show a profit on the statements. This leaves the impression that both management and the accountants have *earned* the profits, which they haven't. Operations people earn the profits for the company through good business systems and procedures. Management must be credited for profits if it provides good systems. The better the

systems and procedures, the bigger the profits. Accountants are there merely to furnish data about the operation's profits.

3. It seems that "outbreeding" has taken the profit instincts away from the accountant's repertoire of business contributions. Years of general ledger work, payrolls, and detailed projects have removed the profit incentive. I've had experience with numerous cases where accountants have stopped profit-maker programs to make room for another general ledger project. In one case my COM program would have paid for a new cost system. Another alternative—a part number principle, short-term-cost program for use as a back up while the long-term-cost system was being installed—was also ignored. They were missing price-increase losses of $2,000 per purchased part per increase at the time.

The accountants dropped profit programs and replaced them with nonprofit accounting programs. This is not unusual; it reinforces the ability to handle accounting responsibilities. All aspects of a profit issue, however, must be considered before changes are made in business systems. Profit instincts should play a major part in such decisions. *Profits must come first.* They must pay for accounting programs.

The Internal Auditor

The internal auditor is the property of the accounting department. This is particularly true at the division level or when the company offices are under one roof. This is not a good policy, however; it does not allow an auditor freedom to express profits, so to speak. Most of the time the auditor is pulled from a systematic examination of functions and given menial tasks such as signing checks or substituting for absent employees.

The corporate office internal auditing staff is more effective than its counterpart in independent offices. They are separate from the duties of the accounting staff. Accounting data is reported to corporate-level executives and division managers. Generally, the division managers are required to respond to faulty systems and procedures audit recommendations submitted by the auditors.

This audit approach has its drawbacks, however. One is the limit placed on the auditor's time. The auditor usually travels to outside plants; thus travel time limits the time available in the field. Usually, two weeks is the amount of time spent at an outside plant. In certain situations, however, the auditor is not limited to two weeks. As a COM profit person, I prefer to spend two months studying a company's operation in order to properly assist the company improve its profits.

Another drawback is the follow-up by plant employees. Valuable recommendations fall to the wayside because local plant personnel often do not carry out an auditor's profit ideas.

The third point is accounting. Much of an internal auditor's time is spent on CPA practices, double-checking accounting entries in financial records. When an accounting staff perform operations-analysis functions, they should come closer to COM profits than any other employees in a corporation. The problem for COM is, however, to separate accounting from operations in audit procedures.

Fourth, audit staffs are still under accounting, even at the corporate level. The extent to which a financial vice-president is profit minded will determine how much operations profits will flourish.

Internal auditors belong under the control of an executive vice-president. There they are responsible to the corporation as a whole, not just to accounting. This setup ties the auditors directly to the company president. If this seems impractical, an alternative is to bring in profit people to help the executive vice-president improve profits through systems and procedures.

The Profit Person

The profit person is free from departmental control and from departmental responsibilities. The profit person has only one purpose in a business organization: to make profits.

I have been most successful as a profit person when the corporation president turned me loose. He placed no limits on where I worked, gave me no guidelines. I was left alone—a free spirit—to find additional cash profits in the corporation.

What this meant was that no department was off limits. Anyone who confronted me in reaching my profit goal was, in effect, preventing the company president from reaching the company's profit goal.

The results of this arrangement were impressive. The main reason for my success was that the organizational president or executive vice-president controlled the cash-profits project or program. The program begins at the top of the organizational chart. That is where it must stay to gain the respect it deserves.

The Free-Spirit Approach

Has anyone in your company been given free rein to search for additional cash profits? Has any person been assigned full time to work on the kind of cash problems described in this book?

It is not likely that you will find such a profit person in your company. You may have several employees who qualify as profit people, but they are, first, departmental people. For these employees to get a profit idea out of their departments and into the president's hands is a herculean task.

Why Companies Don't Use a Profit Person

What kind of employee assistance do companies have to guard against profit loss? Companies depend on systems and procedures to control company profits. They hire people to operate the company's systems, using established procedures.

The more responsibilities employees have, the less time they have to control the systems and procedures. This can become so burdensome that controls eventually wear thin, allowing profit losses to slip through the system. The customary remedy is to spend more in wages for additional employees. The alternative is to trade off wages for profit losses in the systems.

The "Law of Employee Responsibility"

Generally, companies refrain from hiring additional employees to fill gaps. The tendency is to give more responsibilities to present employees, thus occupying every working hour of an employee. What this does is remove the possibility of free time for employees to search for profits lost somewhere in the company. I call this practice the "law of employee responsibility."

The law of responsibility is not confined to any one department of an organization. It is present in purchasing, production, quality control, even in accounting.

As a result of this law of responsibility, companies are another step away from hiring a profit person in the organization. The first employee they will hire is a person assigned to handle more responsibilities. Curing the cause of systems problems is secondary.

Most managers find it difficult to understand that a profit person is more valuable than a productive "responsibility employee." This is understandable; most managers are also dominated by the law of responsibility. Even they are not able to see systems and procedures as a whole. Such an outlook tells us why employees cannot take on the responsibility of the magnitude of a COM program, as well as why the responsibility cannot be entrusted to a separate department.

The law of employee responsibility is the reason why profit persons are not found in business organizations. Even if a company has good intentions, the law will eventually catch up with the company. Occasionally, however, there is an exception—the companies that have installed a cash operations management program in their profit-control operation.

The COM program is designed to overcome the law of responsibility, as well as the department's responsibility, by gaining a position for itself at the top of the organizational chart. It is the president, the top profit person in the company, who must support this program for new cash profits through improved systems and procedures.

13. How You Can Set Up Your Own Cash Operation Management Program

The COM program is generated from the top. Top management people are the ones who will make it go. These people include the president, the executive vice-president or general manager, and any other executive with authority over all departments of the company. Under no circumstances should the program be turned over to a particular departmental vice-president or department head. One department head cannot make a decision concerning procedures in another department. The COM program involves decisions from every department.

Let us assume that the president takes on the reins of the cash operations management program. The short-term goals are:

Determine whether cash operations management systems have cash profit weaknesses, and, if so, what the weaknesses are costing the company in gross profits

Attempt to retrieve lost cash through COM program procedures

Put a stop on systems problems that are costing dollars

Developing the plan further, the company president must choose a leader for the COM program and a team of select individuals to carry out the program. This is where the questions begin. Let us look further for the answers that will bring needed profit dollars.

The Cash Operations Theory

The success of a COM program depends on understanding the theory behind it, that COM dollars become lost in the operational areas of the business. These are physical dollars, those not controlled by the departmental system of an organization.

I must emphasize that these dollars escape accounting-coded dollar controls. Accountants are not aware of such losses any more than engineers or salespeople are. These are cash dollar losses falling through operations systems—below the cash management level-line.

How a COM Program Is Originated

How does one put together a complete COM program in a business organization? Who should handle the program? How is it conducted? When can it be instituted? What authority and priorities should be given to the cash operations management program in your own organization?

We will begin by seeking answers in the preceding chapters. This book provides numerous examples of COM problems. There are many ways that cash profits can be lost in a business, and, of course, all of them could not be covered. Systematic procedures, however, have been described, as well as ideas that can lead to the discovery of major profit problems. In this chapter, I suggest several alternatives that can be used to search out these problems in your company.

The Search for Profits

Let us use a question format to explore the mechanics of the program. I have provided questions to assist in locating problems in the plants and to help you decide what to do once they are discovered. The questions are adapted from chapters 4 and 5. This approach should help clarify the COM program with respect to how a consultant looks for profit dollars.

Testers, Profits, and Dollars (Chapter 4)

How did I know where to look? The initial problem with the testers was to find a reason for paying an invoice of $12,600 worth of testers. Since this affected Purchasing and inventory control, I knew these were the areas which should have the most knowledge about the product purchased. As we moved through the chapter, we learned of new areas where "cash dollars" could be found.

How did I know where to start to look? I knew I had to start an investigation when I saw how $12,600 had been ignored in the systems for a period of six months. Such a sum should not be ignored in a business organization.

What made me suspicious of a certain functional area? The fact that billings were not sent to customers alerted me to follow up on inventory control of finished products.

How did I examine the one I selected to give top priority? This billing problem was followed up by recovering statistics manually on shipments to outside client plants. Once the total number of units were identified at each plant, the plant was asked to account for its units. They were either in inventory, in salespeople's hands, or they had been shipped to customers. If the units had been shipped, I requested an invoice billing number for use in tracing back to receivables. If there was no billing number, I instructed the plant people to issue an invoice to the customer.

How I solved the problem. My main responsibility was to account for each $285 unit put in process in the project. This was done by using a manual multicolumn worksheet to determine the status of all 1,000 units we were concerned with. The additional problems fell out of the system as a result of accounting for the quantity and the values on the basic number of testers.

What I recommended. I suggested that thorough reviews be conducted through payables and purchasing procedures. In addition, I asked for a better security system, an audit of billing, a review of and improvement of freight procedures, better reject policies, and, most important, inventory control numbers for every purchased and manufactured sales product.

There were many cash-operations problems in the testers project. The deficiency that stands out as the most destructive, however, was the failure to include a part number on an inventory product.

"The Brain of a Computer" (Chapter 5)

How did I know where to look? An interview with a responsible employee about an aspect of some operation led me to the problem of paying invoices too soon. The interview questions were typical audit checks on the area reviewed.

How did I know where to begin? When a business transaction appears unusual, I immediately know where to start an intensive investigation. This happened with the $165,000 invoice, which was paid ahead of time. It lost $7,150 in cost of money.

What made me suspicious of a certain area? The value of cost of money, due to paying the $165,000 invoice too soon, alerted me to the overall corporate procedure and controls for total cash disbursements.

How did I examine the one I selected to give top priority? I used both manual and computer information to accumulate the specific cash-disbursement facts that led to the $100,000 profit loss.

How I went looking to solve the problem. Initially I submitted the problem of the $1.2 million overpayment to management, whereupon I received all the attention I needed to submit my primary recommendation, which was to instruct the computer to pay on due dates.

What I recommended. A new due-date system was recommended that would give control of cash disbursements back to management.

Selecting a Leader

Who Should Be in Charge? The key to a successful COM program is to use a leader who is knowledgeable and well informed about business systems. This person should be a proven achiever and should have a broad, diversified background in all parts of an organization. He or she should have no political alliances in the company and should not be biased about any aspect of the business. The sole interest of this person should be to contribute profits and profitable ideas. Most of all, it should be understood that the leader must be a good manager of employees and a good organizer of business systems.

Actually, there is no ideal person within a company, because employees tend to be specialists in their own areas. This is to be expected. The inside person I would probably recommend is an experienced systems analyst. This is someone with two or more years' experience in the company, someone who has already established rapport with the department heads.

My second choice for the job would be a manager of internal auditing or a likely successor to that manager. Experience in this position exposes employees to all parts of the business. Do not, however, overlook the possibility of hiring from outside.

The Leader—Permanent or Part Time?

Making the COM program leader position a permanent one depends on the success of the program. The percentages indicate that this will, indeed, become a permanent position. We merely touch on the area here, but, surprisingly, it is an area often overlooked by management. The program thus becomes a permanent necessity in nearly every business organization.

Once management people see the benefits of a COM program, they are likely to hold on to it. Because a new position should be under the jurisdiction of the company president, a new position would result for ensuring continued control and improvement possibilities of overall cash profits. The new position needs to have a direct line from the president or executive vice-president, depending on the size of the company. Hundreds of thousands of profit dollars may be maintained annually by this position. Because it will demand the interest and respect of the highest profit person in the company, great care should be exercised in selecting the person to fill the position.

The Leader's Responsibilities

The leader's first responsibility is to dedicate himself or herself to finding cash profits. Wherever cash is flowing through the company is where profit research should be conducted. Other responsibilities essential to the COM program are given below, along with an explanation of what is expected.

1. *Identify the systems problems.* What visible evidence is there that reveals a systems problem? In Chapter 6, grinding wheels were scattered throughout the plant. In Chapter 9, boxes were stapled precariously. In Chapter 11, envelopes invoices were paid without receipt of materials. Systems problems better concealed were invoices paid ahead of time in Chapter 5. Even the CPAs missed this in their review. In Chapter 4, lost testers went through the complete company purchase and sales system without being billed to customers. In Chapter 12, an additional 12,000 invoices were put through the processing system at a cost of $1.3 million annually in processing costs. A cash-management point to keep in mind is that each problem had grown from relatively minor functions to major dollar problems because of multiple variances in the system. They were multiline product transactions. This type of systems problem can open new profit areas. Methods used to discover problems are based to some extent on common sense, as well as on concentrated observation of detailed analysis work.

2. *Conducting the COM program profit procedures.* I use a number of profit ideas in my reviews as shortcuts to profits. Here are a few:

Go for the "big money"; time will eat up the small money.

What is your company doing with its cash in operations? Run checks and analyses on money spent through disbursements or billed through receivables—by vendor and by customer according to their volume. Are there any exceptional transactions that appear strange to the system?

Follow up on payables and receivables transactions. Are the employees in this area conscientious? Do you trust their interest in their work? Check on the transactions of those you think may be doing inadequate work.

Item-by-item product control works for inventories; it will also work for locating profit losses. Make use of the idea, both in purchasing and in billing.

3. *Define the systems cash problems.* Relate profit findings to management people as promptly as possible. This allows for immediate changes of profit errors going wrong in systems. It will also keep management up-to-date on the program. Here are a couple of helpful hints:

Explain your findings clearly, to ensure that every question that arises in the future can be answered as fully as possible.

The key to large-profit problems is to go for the high-dollar-volume systems areas. Even if you're half wrong, the values will still not be insurmountable.

4. *Suggest recommendations.* Success in finding cash systems problems will be rewarded only when you recommend solutions that solve the new found problems. Numerous recommendations are likely to come from this COM program. Get your profit message across to management with sufficient documentation to support each deficiency that falls from the system. This will also be necessary to make your point with outside companies, vendors, and customers.

5. *Implement recommendations.* Industrial and commercial business organizations across the United States have file drawers stocked with consultant and audit reports loaded with recommendations to improve their business systems. The problem, however, is that the management people in these companies practically never make the effort or do not have the capability of implementing the recommendations into their systems. This is the importance of the COM program. In this cash profits program, problems are solved in the process of recovering cash or revealing systems errors. An operations program is such that you are at the root of your problems when they are found. The idea is to implement the solution while you are still at the point of prevention. The COM program is designed to do this for you, with the appropriate number of hours expended.

Setting Up the Team

The COM program team must be made up from the various departmental areas represented in the program, namely, marketing, engineering, production, purchasing, and accounting. Obviously this is done so that you have a spokesperson from each department.

The staff can be made up of various combinations of employees in the company. For the most part, members of the team will be on temporary assignment, and some of those for part-time analysis work only.

Whom to Select

The COM program leader must be cautious in selecting the members of the team. The best person for the job is the employee in the department who shows the greatest interest in the COM program. Why? Because that person is likely to be a profit person.

Some employees really do not believe there are additional profits to be found in their areas of the company. They can still be good employees, however, because they are good producers of work and they take care of their job responsibilities; but they won't be particularly good profit people. As I have consistently explained in this book there is a difference.

The profit person will have intensive drive or interest in saving profit dollars for the company.

Let me give you an example of a search I made to select members for a COM team. I screened some employees in a marketing department of a large corporation. At the same time that I was screening employees, I brought along some questionable billing items to get some information about their marketing procedures.

Out of five employees interviewed in the marketing department, all gave good answers to my questions. There was one young woman, however, who went a step further than the others. She asked me questions about my consultant program. When I explained my profit approach, she replied with a thought-provoking comment: "If you want more profits, or want to find lost money, this is the place to find it. I've seen some invoices billed out of this department that had huge errors on them."

This comment, of course, deserved following up, but let's stop for the moment. This was exactly the interest I was looking for in seeking a member for my COM program staff. This employee had profits in mind, as well as the responsibilities involved in handling her job. She was also observant enough to realize that errors were flowing through her department. She would know where to find them promptly. Besides, she has probably wanted, secretly, to investigate this area over a long period.

This is the kind of employee who will do the best job for you on your COM program. The idea is to select one or two employees, depending on how many you need for the job, from each of the five areas listed above. Obviously, you too, want to review the employee for appearance, personality, record, and so forth.

Another suggestion is for you to include an internal auditor, or at least an employee with auditing experience, on your COM staff to represent the accounting department. An auditor is already acquainted with the structure of your company—another shortcut for the program. It is important that you select a profit person here also. Most internal auditors are checkers of inventories and accounting codes. These are the accountant auditors. What you need for the COM program is operations analyst auditor, one with a proven record in operations review work for the company.

The Staff Employee's Role

The approximate number of hours alloted to the COM program should be 2,000 to 3,000. This number will fluctuate, depending on the condition of the systems in the departments. Another factor is the size of the company in question. The hundred-million dollar company should fall in the 3,000 hour range; the billion-dollar company must adjust the size of its staff according to its needs.

The members on the staff will initially be expected to give full-time consideration to the profit program. Once the program is underway and information input is calculated and put through analysis, time allocation will become clearer. If there are big problems in the systems, more time will be needed to solve the problem, for cash recovery, or to improve the system.

The line of authority for each staff member goes through the COM program leader. Each staff member will represent his or her departmental section. When a problem becomes apparent, the program leader and the appropriate staff member process the work together. The staff leader, as mentioned, will have a direct line to the company president or the executive vice-president. Once the staff members are pulled from their departments, their departmental managers must give up jurisdiction over them, at least temporarily. The COM program leader is responsible for that employee's hours until termination of the staff member's part in the program. Should the staff member find that his or her obligations require only part-time attention, it will be at the program leader's discretion to send the member back to his department on a temporary basis.

The strength behind such an approach is that each employee is given the chance to work on the departmental functions that they have always desired to work on, that of stopping cash losses. These employees are held back from completing accomplishable tasks in their regular work hours, because they had no direction or program to follow, or, more realistically, the task or tasks were not allowed in their normal jobs.

Summary

A successful cash operations management program is a cluster of profit-making ideas put to work by innovative, interested employees. These ideas must start at the top of your company. They must be started by your company president, who triggers the program for your COM program leader and staff. From that point on, the improvement of your cash operations systems will be in the hands of your company employees. They are the people who know what is wrong in your company operations, right down to the last widget maker.

Final Message

This book is intended to illustrate how profits from within a business organization can add needed financial support to your business operation. The high cost of everything—from the cost of money to the cost of materials is a burden on business management people. These costs are three or four times as much as they were only recently. It makes sense for business organizations to strengthen and improve their cash operations management systems and procedures *within the company*.

If companies are to keep pace with today's inflated prices, they must look elsewhere than to price increases to improve their profits. The internal improvement of cash operations management, as illustrated in this book, has offered an excellent alternative to the corporation's annual financial picture. This is a thinking person's profit program. Employees in every department of a company should be given think time in which to assist you in reaping profits from within for corporate financial success.

INDEX